Maths puz

JOHN DAVIS and
SONIA TIBBATTS

TEACHER
TIMESAVERS

Published by Scholastic Publications Ltd,
Villiers House,
Clarendon Avenue,
Leamington Spa,
Warwickshire CV32 5PR

© **1994 Scholastic Publications Ltd**
Text © **1994 John Davis and Sonia Tibbatts**

Authors John Davis and Sonia Tibbatts
Editor Jo Saxelby-Jennings
Assistant editor Joanne Boden
Series designer Joy White
Designers Micky Pledge and Lucy Smith
Illustrations Liz Thomas
Cover illustration Frances Lloyd
Cover photograph Martyn Chillmaid

Designed using Aldus Pagemaker
Processed by Pages Bureau, Leamington Spa
Artwork by Lynda Murray
Printed in Great Britain by Clays Ltd, Bungay, Suffolk

British Library Cataloguing-in-Publication Data
A catalogue record for this book is
available from the British Library.

ISBN 0-590-53135-2

The right of John Davis and Sonia Tibbatts to be identified as the
Authors of this Work has been asserted by them in accordance with the
Copyright, Designs and Patents Act 1988.

Contents

Introduction

The chief purpose of this book is to provide teachers with a set of easy to use and well-organised activities based on the programmes of study outlined in the National Curriculum maths documents. The activities are not intended to represent a schematic approach to mathematics teaching in the primary school, but will provide back-up materials, extension work and support for other sources being used.

The activities lay a heavy emphasis on the problem-solving, investigative approach which is so essential to meaningful learning in mathematics. The idea of investigation is fundamental both to the study of maths itself and also to an understanding of the ways in which maths can be used to extend knowledge and to solve problems in many fields.

Through these activities teachers will be able to:
- introduce new skills and concepts;
- encourage the children to practise skills in the manipulation of numbers and symbols;
- consolidate/reinforce an idea which has been previously grasped;
- demonstrate the possibility of using ideas/information in a new situation;
- add elements of flexibility to their maths teaching;
- gain some indication of the children's current level of attainment;
- assess whether children are developing positive attitudes to maths.

Organisation

Each page comprises of a photocopiable worksheet which may be worked on by an individual child or it may be more appropriate for it to be completed by a small group of children. It is important that discussion takes place between the teacher and children at all stages and that teachers should be willing to explore new avenues suggested by the children.

All the worksheets can be completed using resources and equipment which are readily available in the classroom. Since at Key Stage 1 particularly the emphasis should be on practical activity, the children should be encouraged, where necessary, to use real apparatus.

Some of the sheets have follow-up suggestions to show how the tasks outlined can be enriched. The teachers' notes also give brief details of additional information and extension tasks and give an indication of the National Curriculum level at which the activity is aimed.

All the tasks involve using and applying mathematics. This requires the children to select the materials they need, use and interpret mathematical terms, present results in a clear and organised way and give justification for the solutions to their maths problems.

Against this background, this book is divided into four sections: Using number; Number patterns; Shape, space and measures; and Handling data. The weighting towards number reflects the importance it is given in the National Curriculum documents.

To cater for the wide range of ability found in the primary school class, the activities in each section are arranged in increasing order of difficulty. At the beginning of each section of the teachers' notes it is indicated how the activities relate to the programme of study for each key stage. There are some tasks involving early Key Stage 3 work (Level 6) which would be suitable for the most able children.
❏ denotes extension activities.

About the authors

John Davis and Sonia Tibbatts are primary school teachers of many years experience. Sonia Tibbatts is a maths specialist and deputy head. John Davis is head of Key Stage 2 in his present school and has

lectured on professional studies courses at Bath College of Higher Education and the University of the West of England.

Using number

Key Stage 1, pages 13–30;
Key Stage 2, pages 19–45.

Flower power (Level 1) This activity is an easy introduction to the number sequence 1 to 10.

Dotty picture (Level 1) This activity also concerns the number sequence 1 to 10.

Fishy business (Level 1) The children could rearrange toy fish, thus gaining an understanding of number conservation.
❏ Increase the numbers of fish and sets. Also allow the children to suggest their own 'rules', such as how many fish swim away and so on.

Fields (Level 1) Through this activity, the children can investigate the number bonds making 5. Ideally, they should be allowed to use toy animals to do this activity practically.

Guessing game (Level 1) An alternative version of this game could be to use a blank die, which can then be numbered as required, rather than the number cards. You may wish to have the range from 3 to 10.
❏ Increase the numbers on the cards or die as the children's estimating skills develop. For older children, use two dice. Then they can calculate either the sum or the product and play a similar game.

Fruit stall (Level 1) This activity involves counting and recording.
❏ If prices are included for the fruit, then the children can make their own shopping lists and total the bills.

Bull's-eye (Level 2) In this activity, the children investigate the totals that can be achieved by adding three numbers. *Answers:* 30; 3; 27, 6.

❏ What other scores can they get if only one dart can land in each number? Are there any scores they can't get like this? 'Double' and 'treble' rings could be added to the board for more able children, making this a Level 3 activity.

Some sums (Level 2) This investigation involves finding different ways of achieving the total 20 using the four number operations.

❏ This activity can be used with any total and the conditions can be changed in order to practise different number operations. Some children will be fascinated to discover that there are an infinite number of sums, which it is worth spending some time discussing.

Lollipops (Level 2) The children may need to use a calculator and/or coins. You may choose to limit the number of lollipops they can buy, they would then have 'change'.

❏ The amount that each child has to spend can be changed to cater for a range of abilities.

Money matters (Level 2) The children will need to use coins for this activity, and be encouraged to find all the possible alternatives.

❏ Investigate other values of coins in the same way. It may be necessary to place a limit on the number of coins that can be used; for example, 'Make 25p using exactly three coins.'

Number routes (Level 2) Some children may need calculators and they should be encouraged to record their workings. *Answers:* 4, 3, 7; 9, 3, 7, 5 (24); 3, 5 (8).

❏ Can the children design a route with an infinite number of solutions?

Dicey digits (Level 3) The children are required to order numbers and need to understand that the position of a digit indicates its value.

Mystery number crossword (Level 3) This puzzle gives practice in writing number names.
Answer: seventeen.

Times bingo (Level 3) Allow the children to use a calculator or a tables square initially. As their skill develops, you may introduce an element of competition. Encourage the children to invent their own games and make up their own 'rules'.

❏ You may choose to limit this activity to one set of multiples (for example, the two times table). The children should make suitable bingo cards, throw either one or two dice and multiply by the given number (for example, 2). The game can also be extended to include probability – which numbers will occur most frequently?

Reducing squares (Level 3) The children can investigate corner numbers of all sizes.

❏ What is the highest number of squares? Introduce negative numbers.

Best guess (Level 3) Vary this game according to the ability of the children playing by changing the sums. The children need to understand about 'rounding numbers'. The most important point is for the children to develop estimating skills and to be able to use a calculator to check approximations.

❏ A similar activity may be developed using other 'sums' – multiplication, division and so on.

Pyram-adds (Level 3) The children may want to establish 'rules' for using numbers in the pyram-add diagram, such as whether a number can be repeated. *Answers* (for example): >50 = 7, 7, 7, 8, 8, 8, 9, 9; <25 = 2, 3, 2, 3, 2, 3, 2, 3; >80 is not possible as 80 is maximum; 46 = 5, 5, 6, 6, 6, 6, 6, 6.

❏ Extra rows could be added to the pyram-add. Let the children devise their own challenges.

Book fair (Level 3) Calculators may be needed.
Answers: Joanne could buy *Creepy Tales* and *Short Stories 1* or *2*; Sam could buy, for example, *Short Stories 1* or *2*, *Puzzle Book*, *Sticker Book 1* or *2* and *Tree Spotter*; 36p.

❏ The amount each child in the puzzle may spend could be increased. Then the children could

calculate the total value of the books which these pupils could buy.

Adding decimals (Level 4) First, the children should be given practice in adding whole numbers within this box system. *Answers:* (3 × 3) 9.6 and 21.3; (4 × 4) 20.2 and 24.2.

❏ Make the decimal numbers more difficult by using tens and hundredths.

Using bonds (Level 4) Some general revision of number bonds may be necessary. The larger the number the more permutations there will be. As work progresses, the children may be able to predict the results likely to give the largest product without having to write down every solution.
Answer: the greatest product of 6 is 9.

❏ The children could try to find the greatest products for all the numbers from 1 to 20. Are there any patterns?

Magic squares (Level 4) Versions of the original squares should remain 'magic' providing the same rule is applied to all the numbers.

5	10	3
4	6	8
9	2	7

Total = 18

17	22	15
16	18	20
21	14	19

+12 total = 54

10	20	6
8	12	16
18	4	14

×2 total = 36

-2	3	2
5	1	-3
0	-1	4

Total = +3

10	35	30
45	25	5
20	15	40

Total = 75

❏ Let the children devise other magic squares. They could try 3 × 3 squares using just the digits 1 to 9 once only or make larger 4 × 4 and 5 × 5 squares.

Crafty corners (Level 4) In order to check quickly the answers to the multiplication sums using larger numbers, it may be advisable to let the children use a calculator.

Answers: 2 × 6 and 3 × 4 = 12; 6 × 18 and 9 × 12 = 108.

❏ Try larger squares and rectangles. If space becomes short, overlap the shapes.

Make 57 (Level 4) Players should be encouraged to think ahead especially near the end of the game. Developing some kind of plan or strategy is recommended, rather than haphazard choices.

Finding primes (Level 4) It is important that each striking out activity is done carefully, otherwise some prime numbers may be wrongly identified. Remind the children that some numbers may be marked more than once, for example 6 (in the two times and three times tables).

Dartboard (Level 5) *Answers:* there are 14 ways of making 50 with three darts. On the second board, the smallest score is 4 and the largest score is 80.

❏ Encourage the children also to tackle tasks involving 'trebles', the inner bull (50) and the outer bull (25).

A-maze-ing (Level 5) The number mazes shown use times tables (multiples of 4, 6 and 7).

Answers (there may be others!): 4, 96, 108, 924, 172, 492, 220, 168, 432, 444; 6, 216, 690, 474, 492, 294, 108, 96, 408, 384, 78, 168, 372, 114, 66; 7, 35, 28, 392, 455, 602, 861, 742, 763, 504, 378, 63, 287, 77.

❏ Use other number families in similar mazes, for example odd and/or even numbers, square numbers or prime numbers.

Number chains (Level 5) These chains become progressively more difficult although the method of working remains the same. *Answers:* 2, 1, 3, 4, 7; 8, 9, 17, 26, 43; 2, 5, 7, 12, 19; 5, 11, 16, 27, 43; 3, 6, 9, 15, 24; 1, 3$\frac{1}{2}$, 4$\frac{1}{2}$, 8, 12$\frac{1}{2}$.

❏ Fractions, mixed numbers and decimal numbers could be used to give variation and extend the task.

Letternumbs (Level 5) This puzzle shows the use of numbers 'beyond the classroom'.

Answers: 1. 18 holes on a golf course; 2. 12 months in a year; 3. 17 letters between B and T; 4. 6 sides of a hexagon; 5. 15 men on a dead man's chest; 6. 11 people in a football team; 7. 3 sides of a triangle; 8. 6 balls in an over; 9. 10 green bottles (standing on the wall); 10. 3 blind mice (see how they run); 11. 57 Heinz varieties; 12. 13 loaves in a baker's dozen; 13. 26 letters of the alphabet; 14. 21 spots on a die; 15. 88 keys on the piano; 16. 13 stripes on the American flag; 17. 64 squares on a chessboard; 18. 15 reds on a snooker table; 19. 40 days and nights of Lent; 20. 200 pounds for passing GO! in Monopoly.

Hangmaths (Level 5) This is a number version of the familiar 'Hangman' spelling game. It might be advisable to start with two-digit numbers while the children get an idea of how the game is played.

Cuckoo in the nest (Level 6) Encourage the children to put all the fractions in each nest into the same fraction family by finding the lowest common multiple. *Answers:* $\frac{5}{8}$; $\frac{3}{9}$, $\frac{4}{9}$; $\frac{9}{16}$, $\frac{6}{70}$.

❏ The same type of activity could be used when dealing with equivalent decimal fractions.

Mix and match (Level 6) At a simple level, the children will need to think about their number bonds to match the shapes. This activity will strengthen their knowledge of tenths and hundredths too. Calculators could be used to double check their solutions.

Answers: 1. 4.2 + 5.3; 2. 7.9 + 6.1; 3. 6.37 + 6.63; 4. 7.9 + 5.3; 5. 8.21 + 9.55; 6. 8.21 + 5.3.

Percentage bingo (Level 6) A game to sharpen up the children's awareness of percentages – out of 100 or parts of 100.

❏ This game could be used with other work on percentages, especially financial dealings, like interest rates, VAT and sale reductions.

Types of fractions (Level 6) Through this activity, the children should be able to convert vulgar fractions into decimal fractions using a calculator and then see the relationship between these two types of fractions and percentages.

Answers: 0.1, 10%; 0.01, 1%; 0.5, 50%; 0.05, 5%; 0.2, 20%; 0.5, 50%; 0.8, 80%; 0.125, 12.5%; 0.25, 25%; 0.375, 37.5%; 0.75, 75%; 0.875, 87.5%.

Number patterns

Key Stage 1, pages 46–55;
Key Stage 2, pages 47–68.

Calculator patterns (Level 1) This activity will develop familiarity with the calculator.

Snakes and ladders (Level 2) The children should have access to counting materials and should be encouraged to talk about the number patterns, particularly the ones they devise themselves.

Answers (there may be more!): 2, 4, 6, 8, 10, 12; 9, 10, 11, 12, 13, 14, 15, 16, 17; 10, 12, 14, 16, 18, 20, 22, 24; 5, 10, 15, 20, 25, 30, 35, 40, 45; 3, 6, 9, 12, 15, 18, 21, 24; 2, 4, 8, 16, 32, 64 or 4, 8, 12, 16, 20, 24.

The puzzled postie (Level 2) This activity must be preceded by some discussion about how houses are usually numbered; that is, odds on one side of the street and evens down the other. It would be useful to give the children a variety of envelopes to sort, numbered accordingly.

Counting calculator (Level 2) This activity demonstrates a useful calculator facility – constant addition.

Colour match (Level 2) Colour factor/Cuisenaire rods will be needed for this activity. Some children will benefit from copying the pattern of the rods on to squared paper. Others may find the use of symbols a difficult concept to master.

Arrowgraphs (Level 2) In the first two examples (+3 and +4), all the numbers are visited once but not in one string, the third example (×2) has several short chains and not all the numbers are visited.

Answers: (+3) 1, 4, 7, 10, 13, 16, 19; 2, 5, 8, 11, 14, 17, 20; 3, 6, 9, 12, 15, 18. (+4) 1, 5, 9, 13, 17; 2, 6, 10, 14, 18; 3, 7, 11, 15, 19; 4, 8, 12, 16, 20. (×2) 1, 2, 4, 8, 16; 3, 6, 12; 5, 10, 20; 7, 14; 9, 18.

Function mazes (Level 3) The children will need previous experience using just one operation in function machines/mazes.

❑ Suggest that the children give a list of 'outputs' from their mazes to their friends to try, in order to develop understanding of inverse operations. Extend this to a Level 4 activity by asking the children to make a table showing their inputs and outputs for each function maze.

Magic dice (Level 3) The children will need to discover that the opposite faces of a traditional die total 7.

Picture value (Level 3) It is interesting to see what strategies children use for this activity. Some will use a trial and improvement method, others will use the information available to calculate the solutions. *Answers:* flower = 2; tree = 3; car = 4; house = 5; ? = 10.

Table patterns (Level 3) Some introductory discussion may be necessary. Explain that the children need to colour the number 2, then count on two squares and colour the next square and so on. Some children will be tempted to predict a pattern too soon!

❑ Go on to look at which numbers are coloured in the different patterns – to lead into an investigation of factors and/or prime numbers.

Egyptian counting (Level 4) Children enjoy working with other number systems as an alternative to the one we have in current usage. *Answers:* 1. 65; 2. 2,431; 3. 50,261; 4. 402,000.

1. ∩∩∩∩ ＼＼＼＼

2. ⌒ ⌒ ∩ ｜｜｜

3. ⌒⌒ ⌒⌒⌒ ∩∩∩∩ ｜｜｜

4. (figures) ⌒⌒⌒⌒⌒ ∩｜｜｜

5. (figures)

6. (figures)

❑ Roman numerals are a popular alternative system often used in school, but there are others such as the Mayan and the Greek number systems.

Crack the code (Level 4) This code is often known as a 'dot and box system'. Once the children are used to the set-up, they may be able to predict the solutions rather than having to read them off.
Answers: MEET ME ON FRIDAY; BRING YOUR CAMPING GEAR; HAVE PLENTY OF MONEY.

1. (code symbols)

2. (code symbols)

Consecutive numbers (Level 4) This should be tackled as a long running investigation. Numbers do not have to be looked at in order – the easiest solutions can be found first.

❑ Investigate the patterns for the numbers from 50 to 100.

Jumping frogs (Level 4) This activity is all about sequence and patterns – two of the key elements in the study of number. Once the children have established the method of working, the permutations are almost endless.
Answers: the rule is '+2, then +3'. The frog will land on 15, 17, 20, 22. Sequences: 18, 21, 25, 28; 24, 27, 33, 36; 31, 36, 43, 48. Next rule is '-3, then -2'. The frog will land on 38, 36, 33, 31.

Square-eyed (Level 4) This is a variation of 'Four in a row' and is not only aimed at getting the children thinking about square numbers, but also at improving their estimating skills.
Answers: $9^2 = 81$; $11^2 = 121$; $17^2 = 289$; $8^2 = 64$; $15^2 = 225$; $24^2 = 576$; $10^2 = 100$; $30^2 = 900$; $13^2 = 169$; $40^2 = 1600$; $25^2 = 625$; $21^2 = 441$; $18^2 = 324$; $7^2 = 49$; $28^2 = 784$; $16^2 = 256$.

Using letters (Level 5) Many number/letter substitutions are needed. *Answers:* 1. 19; 2. 40; 3. 48; 4. 12; 5. 35; 6. 3; 7. 12; 8. 10.
1. 8, 10, 12, 14; 2. 4, 6, 8, 10, 12.

Sequences (Level 5) Once the pattern has been set, future results should be worked out by prediction.
Answers: 1. 31, 36, 41; 2. 37, 30, 23; 3. 27, 31, 34; 4. 41, 39, 34; 5. 2, $2\frac{1}{4}$, $2\frac{1}{2}$; 6. $7\frac{1}{2}$, $8\frac{1}{2}$, $9\frac{1}{2}$; 7. $14\frac{1}{4}$; $13\frac{1}{2}$, $12\frac{3}{4}$; 8. $1\frac{9}{10}$, $2\frac{3}{10}$, $2\frac{5}{10}$; 9. 2.0, 2.2, 2.4; 10. 17.8, 2.4; 10. 17.8, 17.3, 16.8; 11. 17.25, 17.0, 16.75; 12. 1.92, 2.04, 2.16.

❑ Once the set tasks have been completed, there is endless scope for the children to make up their own sequences.

Which key? (Level 5) This is largely a problem-solving task. The children should make reasoned guesses first and only use the calculator to check their predictions. *Answers:* 1. +, ×; 2. −, ×; 3. +, ÷; 4. −, +, 5. ×, ÷; 6. −, ×; 7. ÷, +; 8. ÷, −; 9. ×, −; 10. −, ÷; 11. ÷, ×; 12. −, ÷.

Three jumps to 100 (Level 5) It is important to note that only single digits can be used for the operations. Encourage the children to vary the use of the four signs as much as possible. This can be a very long on-going activity. It might be easier for the children to split into groups and investigate a few numbers each.

Integers (Level 6) Children need to appreciate as soon as possible that the number line extends below 0. This task will also be good preparation for more detailed work on positive and negative numbers. *Answers:* 1. 3; 2. -3; 3. 1, 4, 7; 4. 7°C; 5. 8°C; 6. 2°C.

❑ Collection of temperature records from newspaper weather reports from Britain during winter, or from around the world, will help to reinforce the concept of 'below zero'.

Fibonacci (Level 6) This number sequence has many interesting spin-offs and can easily be continued to allow the children to work with much larger numbers. Look at 'odds and evens' and the differences between consecutive numbers. This sequence occurs often in the natural world, for example in the development of spirals such as snails' shells.

❏ The additional sequence activity should be started with very small numbers (under 10) and build up in difficulty. The results should follow the same pattern.

Pascal's triangle (Level 6)

❏ Look in detail at some of the diagonal lines. For example, there is a line of 1s, a line of the counting numbers and a line showing the triangle numbers. Also look at the differences between the numbers in the diagonals to identify further patterns.

Triangular patterns (Level 6) The exciting thing about this sequence investigation is that three different patterns will emerge simultaneously. To avoid shading, the children can count the triangles pointing down and the triangles pointing up. *Answers:* 1. 4, 3, 1; 2. 9, 6, 3; 3. 16, 10, 6; 4. 25, 15, 10; 5. 36, 21, 15; 6. 49, 28, 21; 7. 64, 36, 28.

Shape, space and measures

Key Stage 1, pages 69–93;
Key Stage 2, pages 78–113.

Animal ears (Level 1) The children could draw their own animal pictures with 'funny ears' and describe them using similar mathematical terms.

Animal magic (Level 1) Encourage the children to think of ways to check which are the longest snake and mouse's tail; possibly using a piece of string.

Car chase (Level 1) The children will need toy cars of similar length in order to try this puzzle practically.

Repeating shapes (Level 1) The children could use two-dimensional shapes to draw around to make the patterns.

Block patterns (Level 1) In order to try out these patterns practically the children will need blocks of uniform size, ideally 2 × 1.

Colour spots (Level 1) The children will need coloured counters for this activity.

Tidy the toy cupboard (Level 1) Some children will need to have the instructions given verbally. The pictures could be cut out and stuck on to the appropriate shelf or drawn in. Before doing this activity, the children should have practical experience of carrying out these instructions.

Robo-shape (Level 1) The mathematical terms 'triangle', 'rectangle', 'pentagon' and 'circle' could be introduced with this activity.

Shape snake (Level 1) The children may use any appropriate three-dimensional shapes for this activity. Encourage them to describe their snakes using mathematical language and introduce terms such as 'cylinder', 'cuboid' and 'pyramid'.

Shipshapes (Level 2) Encourage the children to describe the movement of the shapes, considering rotation, translation and reflection. They could also investigate the symmetry of the various shapes.

Metre maze (Level 2) *Answer:* the shortest route around the maze is 10m with eight right angles.

❏ The children could estimate the lengths of the routes before counting the sections. Can they use the information to predict the lengths of subsequent routes? Encourage them to write down instructions for the shortest and longest routes for someone else to follow.

Jack-in-the-box (Level 2) Allow the children to take apart packaging boxes, so that they become familiar with the various nets used.

Shopping shapes (Level 2) Collect a variety of boxes and containers to discuss their attributes.

❏ Encourage the children to think of different ways of sorting the shapes and representing them on diagrams. (This will lead into a data handling activity.)

Riddle-me-shape (Level 2) You may prefer to limit the children to either two-dimensional or three-dimensional shapes. Encourage them to consider the attributes peculiar to a particular shape. For example, a four-sided shape with four right angles is a rectangle, but the sides must be equal in length if it is to be a square.

Shape pictures (Level 2)

❏ The children should consider the symmetry of the pictures – which ones demonstrate reflective symmetry? To take this puzzle to Level 3, suggest that the children look for lines of reflective symmetry. They may notice that although the patterns are symmetrical, they do not all have the same lines of reflective symmetry.

Halving (Level 2) The children will need squared paper for this activity. Encourage them to investigate non-identical halves. This can lead to some attractive pattern work.

❏ The children can investigate the tessellation possibilities of some of the 'halves'. This activity can be extended to investigate quartering.

Pattern squares (Level 2)

❏ The children could investigate the symmetry of the patterns, making this a Level 3 activity.

My day (Level 3) This activity involves practice with both analogue and digital clocks, as well as an understanding of the 24 hour clock.

❏ The children could calculate how long they spend on different activities throughout the day.

Calendar puzzle (Level 3) It is useful to have current calendars available for the children.

❏ Investigate upon which days of the week the children's birthdays will fall this year, next year and so on. What day will Christmas Day be on?

Compass points (Level 3)

❏ Let the children draw their own designs on 1cm squared paper and write directions for a friend to follow to copy the design.

Shapes in pieces (Level 3) Encourage the children to look for reflective symmetry in the shapes. They are often confused by the parallelogram; the diagonal is not a line of symmetry – the two halves are rotated.

Mirror pictures (Level 3)
❏ The children can go on to draw their own symmetrical pictures, cut them in half and let their friends complete them by drawing.

Birthday presents (Level 3) Use eight cubes, such as Multilink, to make each of the different shapes.
❏ Encourage an investigation into the most economical way of wrapping the parcels. Let the children choose one parcel and try different ways of wrapping it.

Big hand (Level 3) The children will need to experiment with a variety of units before discovering the most suitable.
❏ They could go on to draw around their hands on 1cm squared paper and find the area by counting squares and parts of squares.

Multi squares (Level 3) Encourage the children to compare the sizes of the different squares they have made. Have they found them all? They could tabulate their results.

What comes next? (Level 4) This activity encourages children to look at a sequence of shapes and then to use established patterns to predict what will come next. *Answers:* squares, areas 1, 4, 9, perimeters 4, 8, 12; triangles, areas 2, 8, 18, perimeters 6, 12, 18.

Tiling (Level 4) Initially, the children should cut out the tiles so that they can physically move them around to make shapes. They will need lots, so they could be cut from 2cm squared paper. A decision may have to be made about whether to classify the square as a member of the rectangle family. Ensure that the rectangles are all entirely different. *Answers:* tiles for four rectangles = 24; tiles for five rectangles = 36; tiles for six rectangles = 60; tiles for seven rectangles = 120.

Pentominoes (Level 4) It is important that the 12 solutions are entirely different and not repeats. In fact, only five are given on the sheet and there are seven others.
Answers (there may be more!):

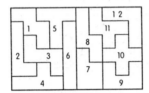 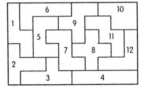

❏ There are many pentomino activities including, for example, using all the pieces to make a fence on squared paper – what is the greatest number of squares that can be enclosed inside? Try activities with hexominoes (six squares) and octominoes (eight squares).

Upside-down (Level 4) Larger 10p coins may be easier for children to handle. *Answer:* the smallest number of moves needed to invert the second shape is 4.

Fraction grids (Level 4) This task suits all children. Solutions can be as simple or as complicated as the children can make them. Strong links here with other topics, such as area and symmetry.

Nets (Level 4) Some children may be able to predict possible solutions and then use maths paper to check. Others may need to resort to paper straight away.

Sizing up (Level 4) This investigation allows the children to compare and establish possible relationships between sets of collected information. There may be some anomalies in the results. In the Egyptian system, 5 digits was about 1 palm and 5 cubits was about 1 stature.

Tangrams (Level 4) There are several other ways of making up the 4 × 4 square and getting a slightly different arrangement of seven shapes.

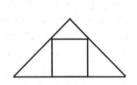

❏ The shapes can be fitted together to make pictures of people, animals, buildings and so on. All seven shapes should be used, touching at some point but without overlapping. All the pictures will have the same area.

Reflections (Level 5)
❏ Extend the activity by making more intricate designs on larger 6 × 6 and 8 × 8 nailboards.

Three in a row (Level 5) This activity has links with games like 'Noughts and crosses' and 'Connect four' and could be played on a competitive basis with the children taking it in turns to place a circle. Reinforce the rule that three in a row are not permitted horizontally, vertically or diagonally.
Answers (for example):

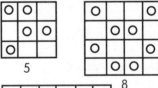 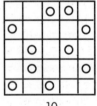

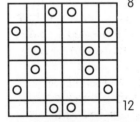 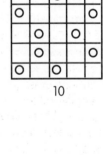

Get the point (Level 5) Make the circles large, otherwise as the number of parts increase the regions become hard to spot. *Answers:* 2 points, 2 parts; 3 points, 4 parts; 4 points, 8 parts; 5 points, 16 parts; 6 points, 31 parts.

Fences (Level 5) Practice in using and explaining the key words 'area' and 'perimeter' may be needed. Point out the possibility of different shapes having the same area and/or perimeter. *Answers:* 1. a 4 p 8; 2. a 4 p 10; 3. a 8 p 12; 4. a 6 p 12 5. a 6 p 12; 6. a 7 p 12; 7. a 9 p 12; 8. a 6 p 14; 9. a 11 p 24; 10. a 12 p 24.

Circle surprise (Level 5) Choosing a wide range of different-sized circles is important in establishing the rule about the circumference being about three times the diameter of any circle. The trundle method can be used to find the circumference of larger circles.

Plotting points (Level 5) This activity will demonstrate the children's understanding of coordinates in all four quadrants. *Answer:* irregular pentagon.
❏ This mapping work can also be used for pattern-making, using one or two lines of symmetry.

Find your way (Level 6) Bearings have practical applications in plotting the courses of ships and aircraft. The children may have to make their own 360° protractors to complete the task. NB: bearings are measured clockwise from N (north) and three-digit answers have to be used, for example, 8° would be 008 and 45° would be 045.
Answers: PQ = 085, 12km; QR = 325, $5\frac{1}{2}$km; RS = 040, 5km; ST = 310, 12km; TU = 190, $6\frac{1}{2}$km.

Möbius band (Level 6) The properties of this band were discovered in 1858 by August Möbius. The dimensions given for the strip are nominal and both the length and the width can be increased. Drawing the line and the colouring both follow one surface without crossing an edge.
❏ Suggest that the children try other bands. What happens if they give a longer strip of paper a full turn (two half turns) and then repeat the investigations?

Making two-dimensional shapes (Level 6)
This activity is all about using the right vocabulary for certain types of triangles and quadrilaterals. Discussion of the terms will be needed before the activities are started.

Towers of Hanoi (Level 6) The rules must be followed rigidly. Strategy is all important and it is a question of whittling down the number of moves until the least number (7) is reached.

Circles in space (Level 6) Plenty of good compass work here, though the dimensions are not fixed. *Answers:* 1. L.Ti.; 2. L.L.; 3. Ti.To.; 4. I.I. (Examples) 1.   2.   3.

Big numbers (Level 6) The purpose here is to give the children a chance to work with some very large numbers in a time setting. A calculator can be used to work quickly and easily or to check answers.
❏ Similarly, the children could also find out and record: how many days there have been since 1 January 1901; how many years there are in 250,000 days; whether one week is longer than one million seconds; whether they could walk one million centimetres in a day; whether they spend one million pence in a year; and how long it would take them to count to one million.

Handling data

Key Stage 1, pages 114–127;
Key Stage 2, pages 119–144.

Shoe muddle! (Level 1) The children could sort piles of shoes practically in the classroom prior to this activity. Encourage them to discuss how they can identify pairs.

Matching up (Level 1) Encourage the children to talk about other pairs of objects that go together.

Which set? (Level 1) The children should decide their own criteria for sorting and should be able to explain their choices.

What next? (Level 1) The children may like to write about the pictures and their predictions. Encourage them to talk about their predictions and help them to realise that different outcomes are possible.

Birthday map (Level 1) This activity can be made into a useful wall display, with the children producing a large scale mapping diagram.

Flaming June (Level 2)
❏ The children can use the data from their weather charts to produce other graphs, such as bar charts. They could make predictions about how many sunny and/or wet days there will be in the month.

Favourite sports (Level 2) Encourage the children to use a tally sheet.
❏ Ask them to suggest questions that they could ask other children about their graphs. Make sure that they can answer them themselves!

Hair and eyes (Level 2) Encourage the children to devise their own data collection sheets and to consider the different ways of displaying data.
Answers: Amy has brown hair and green eyes; Michael has brown hair and brown eyes; Susan has brown hair and blue eyes; Sita has brown eyes and either blonde or black hair and Kate has blue eyes and either blonde or black hair, there is insufficient information to tell which girl is blonde and which is black-haired.
❏ Introduce a third variable, such as sex or age. How can the data be represented?

Pet count (Level 2) You will need to decide together which pets to include.
❏ Use the data as a basis for further graph work. Extend the activity to include other classes. Allow the children to make predictions about other class pets based on the information already collected.

Shape Venn (Level 2) (Links with shape, space and measures.) Initially, limit this activity to the shapes illustrated.
❏ Other shapes can be included to extend the activity. Possibly use three circles in the Venn diagrams, and let the children decide on their own criteria for sorting.

Party time (Level 2) Encourage the use of practical apparatus to investigate the alternative arrangements.

❑ What happens if another family of two children are invited?

Book count (Level 3) The children will need to decide how they will represent the numbers of books for their own book count.

Shape tree (Level 3) (Links with shape, space and measures.) The children may need to write the sorting questions on to cards and physically sort the shapes.

❑ Other shapes could be included; you may wish to mix two-dimensional and three-dimensional shapes. The children should go on to choose their own sorting criteria.

All about me (Level 3) Index cards will be needed. Encourage the children to sort the cards in different ways when searching the data.

❑ Allow them to combine their data with that of other groups to set up a computer database. How does the computer sort the data? Explain the terms 'field' and 'file', if necessary.

Triple cones (Level 3) You may wish to set certain restrictions, such as each scoop must be a different colour. *Answer:* there are ten different combinations of scoops.

❑ Encourage the children to predict how many combinations there will be as extra flavours are added. Can they discover a pattern?

Spinners (Level 3) Emphasise that care must be taken when making the spinners not to bias them. Alternatively, a blank die could be used with coloured spots stuck on.

Fixture list (Level 4) This aspect of handling data involves making as many different permutations as possible. Some children may have to be reminded that teams cannot play themselves. *Answers:* 6; 12; 8; 20; 42; 512.

More or less? (Level 4) Some discussion about the idea of chance may be needed before starting this activity. Emphasise the idea that we cannot be certain what will happen and that we can only say what we think will be more or less likely to happen. *Answers:* boy; under; no glasses; brothers and sisters; either.

New shoes (Level 4) This activity is essentially about the introduction of the key words 'range', 'mean', 'median' and 'mode'. Encourage the children to think about the implications of collecting such data; stock control, for example. *Answers:* range = 5; median = 9½; mode = 9; mean = about 11.

❑ Encourage the children to find the range, mean, median and mode of classroom data such as collar sizes.

Ready reckoner (Level 4) This system may seem a little outdated in these days of electronic tills, but it introduces children to the important notion of constant proportion – items increasing by the same amount each time. *Answers:* straight line; yes, no money and no chocolate; 110p; about 70g.

Tallying (Level 4) The purpose of tallying is to give a quick and easy way to record large numbers and be able to count them simply. *Answers:* 49; 171; 1.00 pm / 2.00 pm; 8.00 am / 9.00 am; 1.00 pm / 2.00 pm.

❑ This skill could be developed to collect information about the frequency of letters used on a page or in a bird census, for example.

Table repeats (Level 5) This puzzle is largely about looking for patterns in data.

❑ Other investigations might include linking the nine times table to the three and six times tables, or seeking connections between the five and ten or the two, four and eight times tables.

Heads and tails (Level 5) This is a natural progression from the activity called 'More or less?' (page 131). Encourage the children to try to predict how the results might change as the number of tosses increases.

Exchange rates (Level 5) This activity will give the children a chance to convert sterling into other currencies. The figures given are buying rates. *Answers:* 1. 458, 2. 1374, 3. 3664; 1. 155, 2. 542.5, 3. 775; 1. 216.8, 2. 1219.5, 3. 2710.

At the dentist (Level 5) This task involves major elements in the investigative process – making a statement and then deciding on the questions to be asked in order to collect the data needed to help check the statement.

Pie charts (Level 5) Assistance with the divisions is given on the page as the charts are marked with the hours on the clock face.

❑ Children conversant with the 360° protractor may make their own charts. There are also potential links with percentages.

Venn diagrams (Level 6) Some revision of the key words used in this activity may be needed; for example, 'square numbers' and 'multiples'. *Answers:* 25; 20; 28; 15; 6; 4, 16; 9; 36.

❑ Use some of the children's own data, such as hobbies or favourite foods, in Venn digrams.

Happy birthday (Level 6) This is a simple form of scattergraph which will allow the children to place more than one cross in each box.

Curved graphs (Level 6) A complete variation from the norm, as most of the graphs primary children use are made up of straight lines. Good links with area work. *Answers:* area of square 1, 4, 9, 16, 25, 36; 6.25, 12.25, 20.25; 2.23, 3.87, 4.47.

Wonder bar? (Level 6) Whereas many data handling activities ask the children to interpret given data, here they have the chance to initiate their own research.

Pick me up (Level 6) As happens in other activities like this, it should be noted that the larger the number of results collected, the more likelihood there is of getting closer to the ratio of 3:2:1.

Name _____

Flower power

♣ Starting at **1**, follow the lines to join the dots.

♣ Now colour the flower.

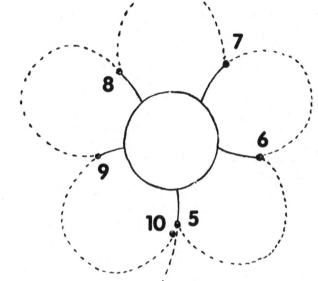

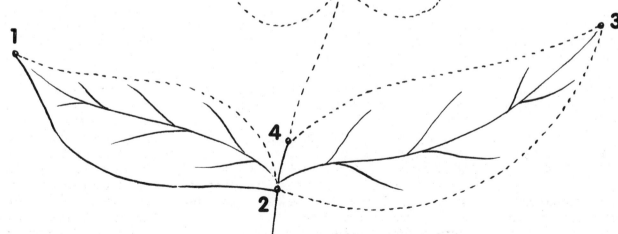

Name _____

Dotty picture

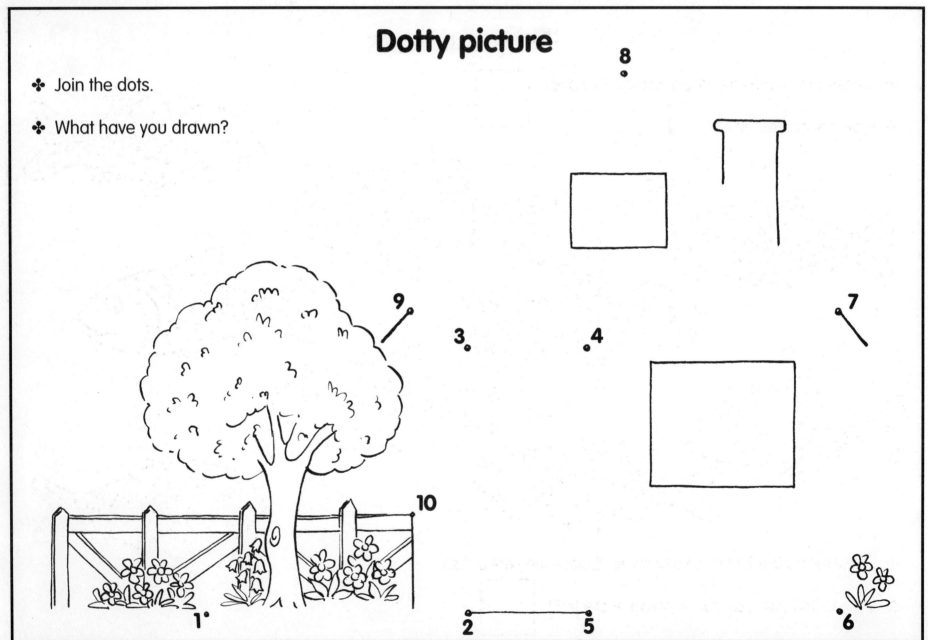

Dotty picture

❖ Join the dots.

❖ What have you drawn?

Teacher Timesavers: Maths puzzles

Name _____

Fishy business

✤ Guess how many fish there are on this page. ☐

✤ Now count the fish. ☐

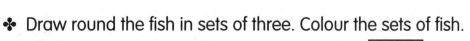

✤ Draw round the fish in sets of three. Colour the sets of fish.

✤ If three fish swim away, how many are left? ☐

Fields

Name _____

Fields

A farmer keeps five animals in each field.

✤ Cut out the sheep and cows and stick them in the fields.

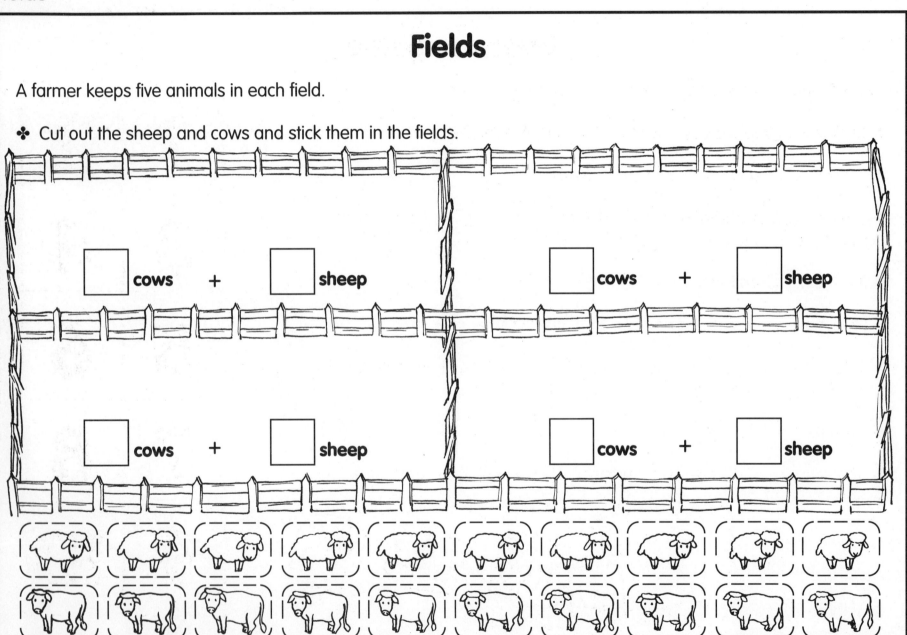

⬜ cows   +   ⬜ sheep

⬜ cows   +   ⬜ sheep

⬜ cows   +   ⬜ sheep

⬜ cows   +   ⬜ sheep

Name _____

Guessing game

You will need: some cubes, a pot and a partner.

✤ Stick the number cards opposite on to card and cut them out.

✤ Put the number cards in a pile face down.

✤ Take a card, and without showing anyone, count out the number of cubes shown on the card and put them in a pot.

✤ Tip the cubes on to the table.

✤ Your partner must guess how many cubes you have tipped out.

✤ Count the cubes together. If your partner guesses right they keep the cubes. If they are wrong, you keep them.

✤ Next it is your partner's turn.

✤ The winner is the player with the most cubes when all the cards have been used.

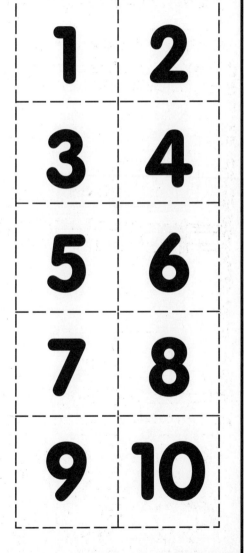

1	2
3	4
5	6
7	8
9	10

Fruit stall

Fruit stall

♣ How many are there of each fruit?

KIWIS

CHERRIES

PINEAPPLES

APPLES

RASPBERRIES

STRAWBERRIES

ORANGES

PEARS

BANANAS

PLUMS

Name _____

Bull's-eye

You have three darts.
Each dart must score.

❖ What is the highest score you can get on this dartboard?

❖ What is the lowest score you can get?

❖ If only one
dart can land in each number:

- what is the highest score?

- what is the lowest score?

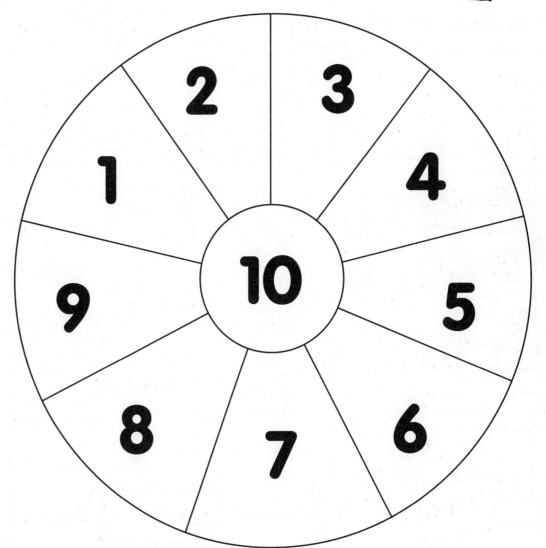

Some sums

$+$ $-$ $\times$ $\div$ **Some sums** $+$ $-$ $\times$ $\div$

✤ Fill in the sums below to give the answer 20.
One is done for you.

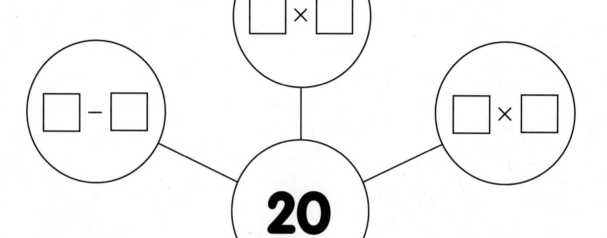

✤ Are there any
more ways of
making 20?

✤ Investigate how
many ways you can make:
- + sums;
- − sums;
- × sums;
- ÷ sums.

Name _____

Amy, Ben, Chris and Raj are going to buy lollipops. The children have 30p each to spend.

✤ How can each child spend 30p in a different way?

Ben

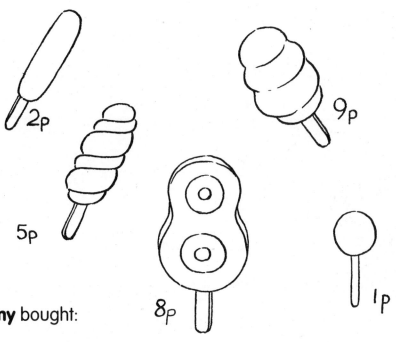

2p

5p

9p

8p

1p

Chris

Raj

Amy bought:

2 × 9p lollipops;
2 × 5p lollipops;
1 × 2p lollipop.

She spent:
9p + 9p + 5p + 5p + 2p = 30p

You may need a calculator to help you.

Money matters

Name _____

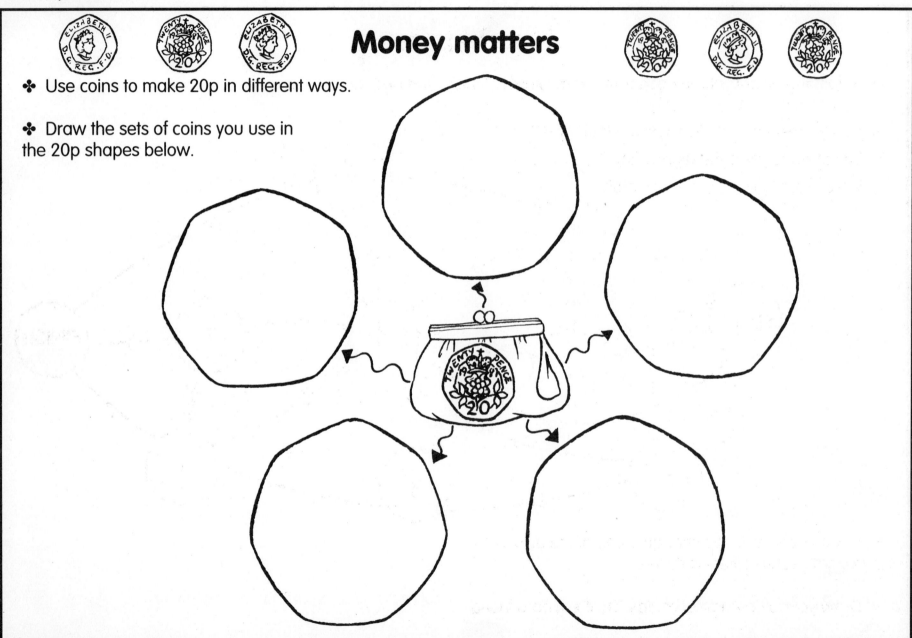

Money matters

♣ Use coins to make 20p in different ways.

♣ Draw the sets of coins you use in the 20p shapes below.

Name _____

Number routes

❖ Follow the arrows along each route from 'start' to 'finish' and add the numbers.

❖ Can you find a route that gives a total of 14?

❖ Which route gives the highest total?

❖ Which route gives the lowest total?

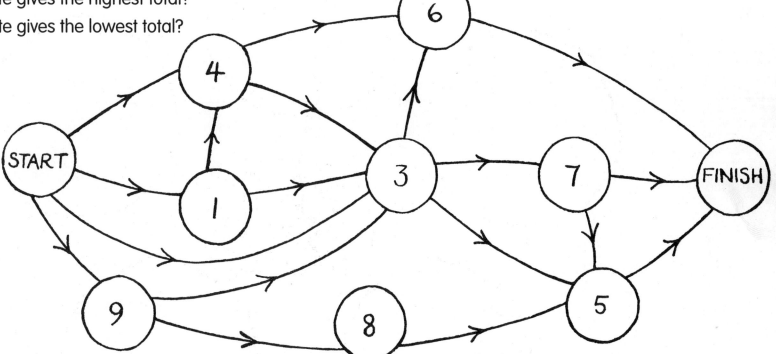

❖ What happens if you change some of the arrows? Investigate some different routes.

❖ Draw your own number routes. Try them on a friend.

Dicey digits

Name _____

Dicey digits

♣ Shamilla and Ben are playing a game. They each roll three dice and have to make a number from the three digits. The highest number wins.

Shamilla

Shamilla makes 543.

Ben

Ben makes 621.

So Ben wins that round!

They record their scores on a chart:

SHAMILLA	BEN
543 ✗	621 ✓

♣ Play this game with a partner. Take it in turns to roll three dice and record your scores opposite.

Name _____

Mystery number crossword

✤ Spell out the mystery number (1 down) by using the clues.

Clues

1 Days in a week.

2 Nine less than twenty.

3 Double six.

4 Two times two times two.

5 The difference between nineteen and twenty.

6 Four fours.

7 Twenty-five less three less twelve.

8 Nine divided by three.

9 Two add six add one.

✤ Now make up a clue for the mystery number.

Times bingo

Times bingo

You can play this game with one or more friends.
You will need: two dice (numbered 1 to 6), some card, pens or pencils and some counters.

❖ Make your own bingo cards.

• Draw a 4 × 3 grid on to a piece of card.

• Colour any one section in each row. Perhaps like this:

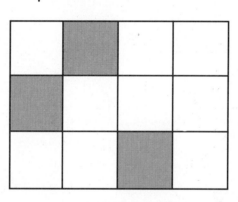

• Choose any nine numbers from the grid below to complete your card.

• Try to make your card different from your friend's card.

1	2	3	4	5	6
8	9	10	12	15	16
18	20	24	25	30	36

❖ The players take turns to:
• roll both dice and work out the product of the two numbers, for example: 4 × 5 = 20;
• cover that square if it is on their bingo card.

❖ The winner is the first player to cover all their bingo card numbers.

❖ Are some numbers a better choice for your card than others?

❖ Invent some other multiplication games using the dice and your bingo cards. What are the rules?

Name _____

Reducing squares

This is a reducing square. Whatever numbers you start with, they reduce to 0.

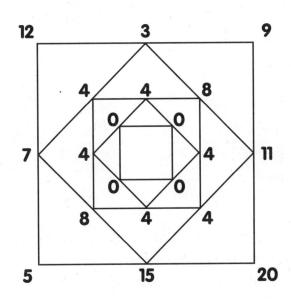

✤ Investigate some reducing squares of your own.
• Put any four numbers at the corners of the outer square opposite.
• Work out the difference between each pair of corner numbers to get the corner number of the next square.
• Find the next four corners in the same way.
• Continue doing this until you get to 0. Add more squares if you need to.

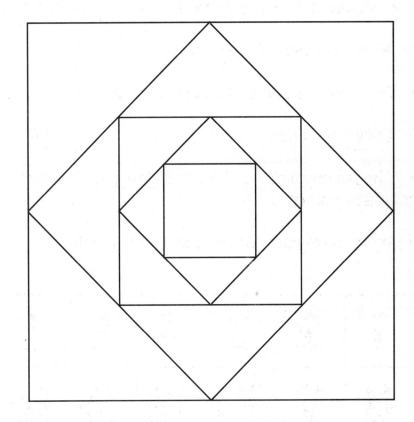

✤ Try using different sets of corner numbers. Do you notice any patterns?

Best guess

Best guess

Here are some sums and some estimates of the answers.

✤ For each sum, decide which you think is the best estimate of the answer, then use a calculator to check.

✤ Write down the true answer. Was yours a good or bad guess?

Sum	Estimates				True answer	Good or bad guess
53 + 28	60	70	80	90		
61 + 32	80	90	100	110		
96 − 31	50	60	70	80		
49 + 22	60	70	80	90		
95 − 48	40	50	60	70		
73 + 58	110	120	130	140		
36 + 16	40	50	60	70		
71 − 49	20	30	40	50		
67 + 58	100	110	120	130		

✤ Now work with a friend.

✤ Think of a sum and write it down.

✤ Let your friend make an estimate of the answer. Then check the answer with a calculator.

✤ Take it in turns to make up sums for each other. Decide how close a guess must be to the true answer to see who wins each round.

✤ Record your game like this:

Sum	Estimate	True answer	Good or bad guess

If your want to, continue on the back of this sheet.

Name _____

Pyram-adds

♣ Choose eight numbers between 0 and 10 and fill in the bottom line.

♣ Add the numbers to complete the boxes in the second line.

♣ Complete the pyram-add.

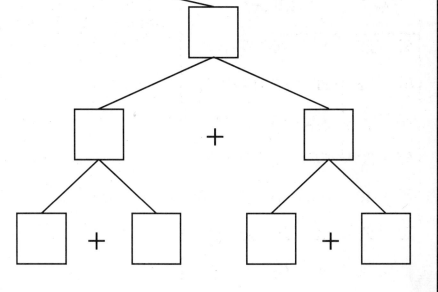

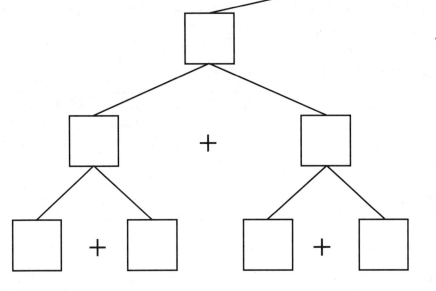

♣ Can you choose numbers to make the top number:
- more than 50?   • less than 25?
- more than 80?   • exactly 46?

Book fair

Book fair

You may need a calculator.

ATLAS £1·95

CREEPY TALES £3·50

SHORT STORIES 1 £1·50

PUZZLE BOOK 65p

BOOK OF KNOWLEDGE £3·99

SHORT STORIES 2 £1·50

FOOTBALL FUN BOOK £2·25

TREE SPOTTER 95p

STICKER BOOK 1 75p

FAIRY STORIES £2·50

STICKER BOOK 2 75p

At the book fair each child has £5.00 to spend.

♣ Joanne buys two books for exactly £5.00. Which books are they?

♣ Sam buys four books and still has change. Which books are they?

♣ Ben buys the most expensive book and the least expensive book. How much change has Ben?

♣ How could Tony, Ajay and Siu Yin spend their money? Decide which books they could buy and how much change they will have. Each child chooses a different selection, but the fair has more than one of each book.

......A.d.d.i.n.g. .d.e.c.i.m.a.l.s. ......

❖ Look at the decimal numbers in this square.

1.8	2.4	
3.2	1.9	

❖ If you add the numbers across and then down, the square looks like this:

1.8	2.4	4.2
3.2	1.9	5.1
5.0	4.3	9.3

What do you notice?

❖ Complete these addition squares. Do they follow the same pattern?

4.8	6.2	
2.7	7.6	

1.9	2.6	
3.7	1.4	

❖ Does the same pattern continue if the squares get bigger?

5.5	1.2	3.1	
0.7	1.6	4.2	
1.7	3.5	2.7	

1.7	3.2	2.5	
2.4	2.1	3.0	
0.9	1.1	3.3	

❖ Try some decimal addition squares of your own. Use a calculator to check your answers.

Name _____

Using bonds

Using bonds

Shown below are all of the number bonds that make 5:

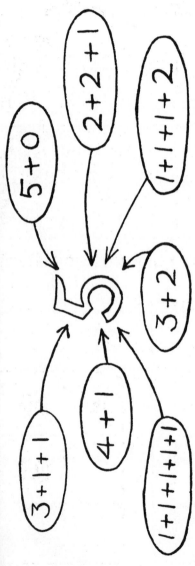

5 + 0

2 + 2 + 1

1 + 1 + 1 + 2

3 + 2

3 + 1 + 1

4 + 1

1 + 1 + 1 + 1 + 1

❧ Which of these number bonds gives the greatest product?
These are the products for the number bonds given above:

1 + 1 + 1 + 1 + 1	→	$1 \times 1 \times 1 \times 1 \times 1 = 1$
4 + 1	→	$4 \times 1 = 4$
1 + 1 + 1 + 2	→	$1 \times 1 \times 1 \times 2 = 2$
5 + 0	→	$5 \times 0 = 0$
2 + 2 + 1	→	$2 \times 2 \times 1 = 4$
3 + 1 + 1	→	$3 \times 1 \times 1 = 3$
but 3 + 2	→	$3 \times 2 = 6$

So **6** is the greatest product.

❧ If we try the number 6:

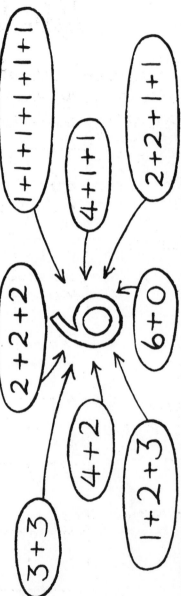

1 + 1 + 1 + 1 + 1 + 1

4 + 1 + 1

2 + 2 + 1 + 1

2 + 2 + 2

6 + 0

4 + 2

1 + 2 + 3

3 + 3

❧ Which bond gives the greatest product now? Use the back
of this sheet to work it out.

❧ Now try some other numbers.

M a g i c   s q u a r e s

Magic squares were devised by the Chinese thousands of years ago. In a magic square each line adds up to the same total.

♣ Complete this magic square opposite.

The magic square total is 18.

5	10	
	6	
		7

♣ Take the same numbers as above and add 12 to each of them.

♣ Is it still a magic square?

♣ Now multiply each of the original numbers by 2. Is it still a magic square?

Will this work for any nine consecutive numbers?

What about negative numbers?

♣ Complete these magic squares.

-2	3	2
	1	
		4

10	35	
	25	
		40

Crafty corners

Crafty corners

1	2	3	4	5	6	7	8	9	10
2	4	6	8	10	12	14	16	18	20
3	6	9	12	15	18	21	24	27	30
4	8	12	16	20	24	28	32	36	40
5	10	15	20	25	30	35	40	45	50
6	12	18	24	30	36	42	48	54	60
7	14	21	28	35	42	49	56	63	70
8	16	24	32	40	48	56	64	72	80
9	18	27	36	45	54	63	72	81	90
10	20	30	40	50	60	70	80	90	100

♣ Look at the top square and rectangle which have been drawn on the table square.

♣ Multiply the numbers in the opposite corners.

- Square: $2 \times 6 =$

  $3 \times 4 =$

- Rectangle: $6 \times 18 =$

  $9 \times 12 =$

♣ What do you notice?

♣ Check your results for the other square and rectangle.

♣ Try the same thing with squares and rectangles of your own.

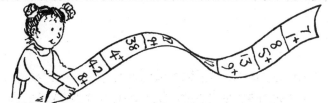

Make 57

For this game you will need: a small counter, a pencil, paper and a partner.

✤ The object of the game is to make exactly 57 or force your partner to make more than 57.

• Put the counter on any number and write the number down on the paper.

• Get your partner to move the counter to any square NOT in the same row or column. For example, with the counter on 6 your partner cannot move it to 3, 7, 9 or 4.

• Add this new number to the first number.

• Play continues in turns, adding each number to the previous one.

• The winner is the player to make a total of 57 or to force the other player to get more than 57.

7	**2**	**5**
3	**1**	**8**
6	**9**	**4**

Finding primes

○○○●○●○●○●●○●○●○●○●○ **Finding primes** ○○○●○●○●●○●○●○●●○

♣ On the hundred square opposite, start from 2 and count in twos, crossing out the numbers as you go – use a black pencil. The first line has been done for you.

♣ Now count in threes starting from 3 – use a red pencil to strike out every third number. Do not cross out 3.

♣ The next unmarked number is 5. Count from here in fives – use a blue pencil to strike out every fifth number. Do not cross out 5.

♣ The next unmarked number is 7. Count from here in sevens – use a green pencil to strike out every seventh number. Do not cross out 7.

♣ Circle the numbers which are left. These numbers are called **prime numbers.**

♣ What are prime numbers? Find out.

1	2	3	4̸	5	6̸	7	8̸	9	1̸0̸
11	12	13	14	15	16	17	18	19	20
21	22	23	24	25	26	27	28	29	30
31	32	33	34	35	36	37	38	39	40
41	42	43	44	45	46	47	48	49	50
51	52	53	54	55	56	57	58	59	60
61	62	63	64	65	66	67	68	69	70
71	72	73	74	75	76	77	78	79	80
81	82	83	84	85	86	87	88	89	90
91	92	93	94	95	96	97	98	99	100

Dartboard

✤ Find all the different ways of making 50 with three darts on the dartboard below. All the darts must score.

This board has a 'double' ring. If a dart lands in the ring it scores twice the usual score.

✤ If one dart scores a double and the other two do not, what is the smallest possible score and what is the largest possible score?

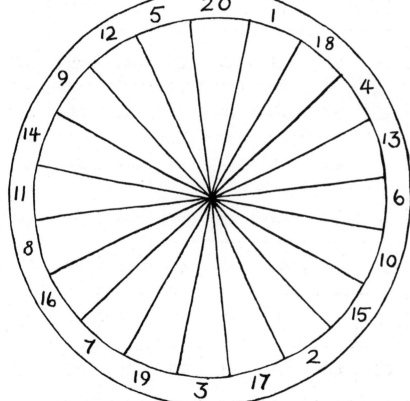

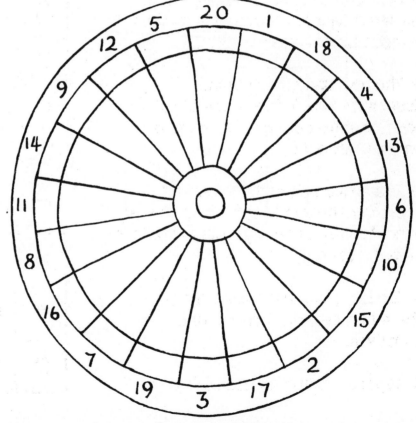

✤ Choose a number larger than 50 and do the same again. Are there the same number of ways?

A-maze-ing

A-maze-ing

❖ Here is a simple maze to 'warm you up'. Can you find a path from the 'start' to the 'finish'?

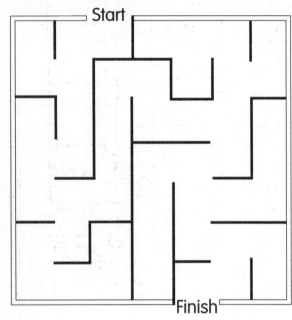

This is a number maze.

❖ Find a path from 4 to 444 using multiples of 4.

6	216	690	724	427	66
74	172	474	274	114	144
924	294	492	220	372	86
108	218	308	87	168	612
96	408	384	78	999	432
4	409	406	774	666	444

❖ Now find a path from 6 to 66 using only multiples of 6.

❖ In the maze below, plot the path from 7 to 77 using only multiples of 7.

7	37	903	609	546	665	840
35	497	679	906	78	588	200
28	433	297	84	693	336	574
97	392	455	385	654	217	777
802	602	583	99	260	321	29
198	861	100	504	378	63	287
19	742	763	49	197	123	77

❖ Invent some of your own number mazes.

Name _____

Number chains

3	4	7	11	18

You get each number in the boxes above by adding up the previous two numbers. For example: $3 + 4 = 7$, $4 + 7 = 11$, $7 + 11 = 18$.

✤ Complete these boxes using the same rule.

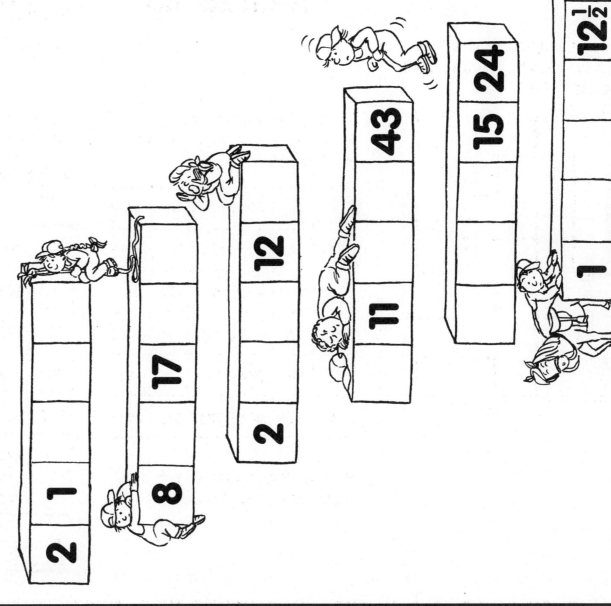

2	1				17		8

2			12

11			43

15	24

1			$12\frac{1}{2}$

✤ Make up some number chains of your own.

Name _____

Letternumbs

Letternumbs

Letternumbs are phrases that use both letters and numbers.
For example: '4 R A in a S' = '4 right angles in a square'.

♣ Try these letternumbs.

1 18 H on a G C _____

2 12 M in a Y _____

3 17 L between B and T _____

4 6 S of a H _____

5 15 M on a D M C _____

6 11 P in a F T _____

7 3 S of a T _____

8 6 B in an O _____

9 10 G B (S on the W) _____

10 3 B M (S H T R) _____

11 57 H V _____

12 13 L in a B D _____

13 26 L of the A _____

14 21 S on a D _____

15 88 K on the P _____

16 13 S on the A F _____

17 64 S on a C B _____

18 15 R on a S T _____

19 40 D and N of L _____

20 200 P for P G in M _____

♣ Can you think of any of your own letternumbs?

Hangmaths

In this game you have to discover all the numbers in a secret sum without being 'hanged'.

✤ One player secretly makes up a sum and shows the other player a blank version.
For example, for:

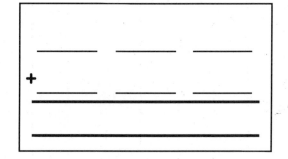

```
  3   4   9
+ 2   7   6
_____
  6   2   5
```

show

```
+  ___  ___  ___

   ___  ___  ___
   _____

   _____
```

✤ Then the other player selects any column
and any digit and asks a question such as,
'Is there a 2 in the tens column?'

✤ If there is, the digit is filled in. If not, part of the hangman picture is drawn.

✤ A player can win by managing to 'hang' his opponent, or by working out the
whole sum correctly before being 'hanged'.

✤ Then the winner has to choose the next secret sum.

✤ Try the same activity using four and five-digit numbers.

Cuckoo in the nest

Name _____

Cuckoo in the nest

Cuckoos lay their eggs in the nests of other birds.

✿ In each of these nests there is one fraction which should not be there.
All the others are equivalent fractions. Spot the odd one out!

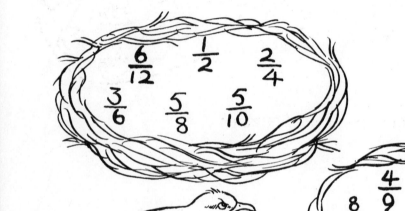

$\frac{6}{12}$ $\frac{1}{2}$ $\frac{2}{4}$ $\frac{3}{6}$ $\frac{5}{8}$ $\frac{5}{10}$

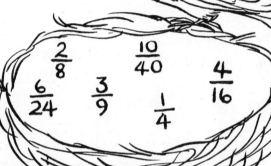

$\frac{2}{8}$ $\frac{10}{40}$ $\frac{4}{16}$ $\frac{6}{24}$ $\frac{3}{9}$ $\frac{1}{4}$

$\frac{4}{9}$ $\frac{2}{3}$ $\frac{10}{15}$ $\frac{8}{12}$ $\frac{12}{18}$ $\frac{6}{9}$

$\frac{5}{50}$ $\frac{4}{40}$ $\frac{6}{70}$ $\frac{1}{10}$ $\frac{3}{30}$ $\frac{2}{20}$

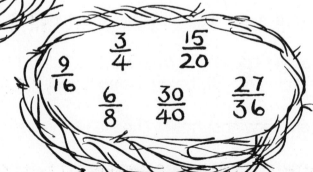

$\frac{3}{4}$ $\frac{15}{20}$ $\frac{9}{16}$ $\frac{6}{8}$ $\frac{30}{40}$ $\frac{27}{36}$

Mix and match

| 4.2 | 6.37 | 1.85 | 7.9 | 8.21 | 4.73 |

(6.1) (3.08) (9.55) (5.3) (6.63) (1.74)

♣ Take one decimal number from the line of squares and add it to one decimal number from the line of circles to complete each of these number sentences below.

1 ☐ + ◯ = **9.5**   2 ☐ + ◯ = **14.0**

3 ☐ + ◯ = **13.0**   4 ☐ + ◯ = **13.2**

5 ☐ + ◯ = **17.76**   6 ☐ + ◯ = **13.51**

♣ Make up some number sentences of your own using the decimals in the squares and circles .

Name _____

Percentage bingo

Percentage bingo

3 of 5

60%

You will need: the bingo cards on this page, pencils, paper and some counters.

✤ The aim is to cover all the percentages on your card with a counter.

✤ To cover a percentage :
- find a statement from the clues to match the chosen percentage;
- tell the statement and the percentage you select to the other player who will check the answer;
- you can only have one go in each turn and each statement can only be used once.

✤ The winner is the first player to cover all their percentages.

Clues			
3 of 10	5 of 25	4 of 16	9 of 12
160 of 320	1 of 10	10 of 50	16 of 20
9 of 30	12 of 24	5 of 20	36 of 48
50 of 500	4 of 80	40 of 50	2 of 40
6 of 120	90 of 120	8 of 40	15 of 60
45 of 90	270 of 900	240 of 300	6 of 60

Player 1

5%	75%	25%	30%
20%	10%	80%	50%

Player 2

5%	75%	25%	30%
20%	10%	80%	50%

Name _____

Types of fractions

$\frac{3}{4}$ can be written as $3 \div 4$.

♣ Use your calculator to turn these fractions into decimal numbers. Then write them as percentages.

Vulgar fraction	Decimal	Percentage
$\frac{1}{10}$	0.1	10%
$\frac{1}{100}$		
$\frac{5}{10}$		
$\frac{5}{100}$		
$\frac{1}{5}$		
$\frac{1}{2}$		
$\frac{4}{5}$		
$\frac{1}{8}$		
$\frac{1}{4}$		
$\frac{3}{8}$		
$\frac{3}{4}$		
$\frac{7}{8}$		

Calculator patterns

✤ Press the ☐1 key on your calculator to make this pattern:

11111111

✤ Now try making this pattern:

12121212

✤ And this one:

11221122

✤ Make a pattern of your own and see if a friend can copy it.

✤ Write it down.

✤ Now let your friend make a calculator pattern for you to copy.

Name _____

Snakes and ladders

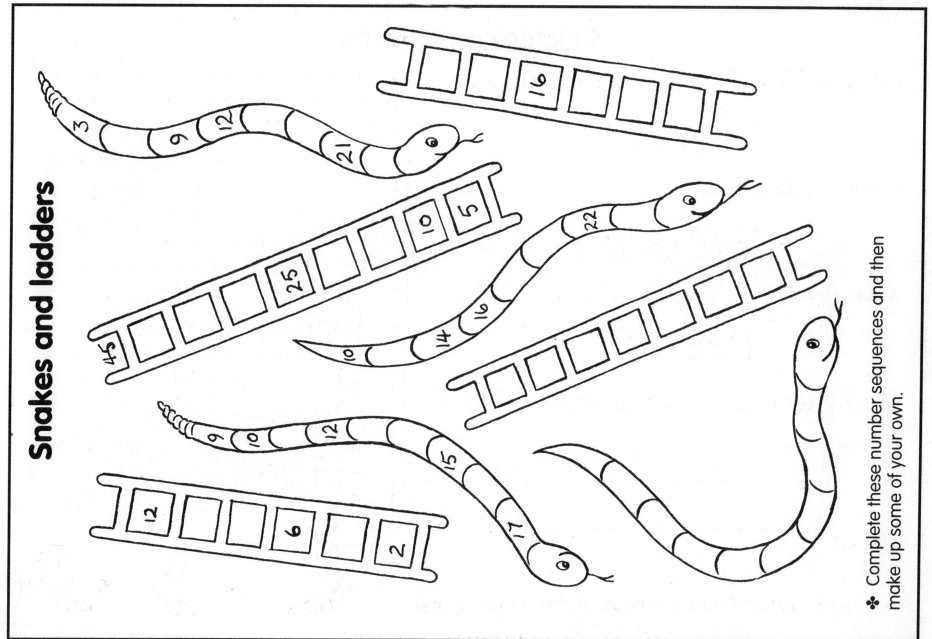

❖ Complete these number sequences and then make up some of your own.

The puzzled postie

The puzzled postie

Can you help the new postie deliver his letters? He will walk along one side
of the road and then back along the other side.

❖ Write the numbers on the houses.

❖ Sort the letters into odd and even numbers and then draw his delivery route.

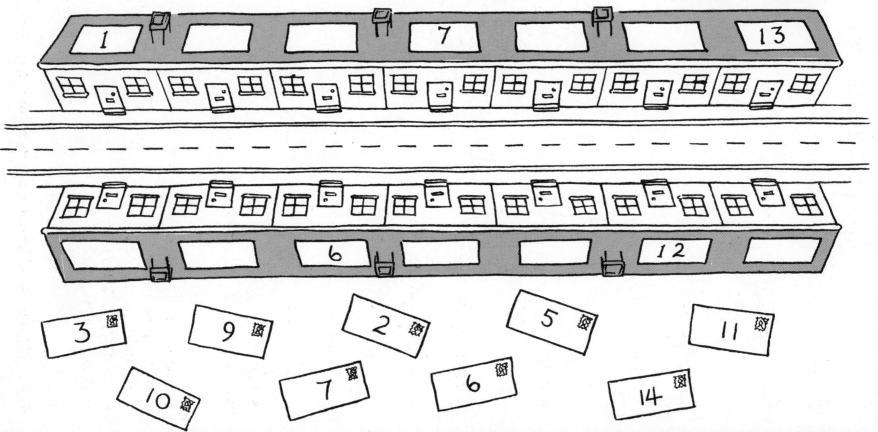

Counting calculator

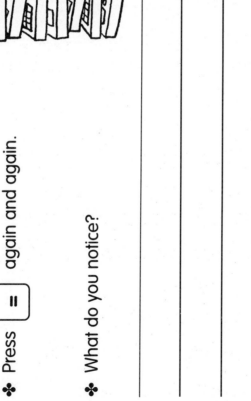

❧ Press these keys on your calculator:

| 1 | + | 1 | = | = |

❧ What shows on the display?

❧ Press | = | again and again.

❧ What do you notice?

_____

_____

_____

❧ Can you make the calculator count in twos?
Record the keys you press.

❧ Can you make the calculator:
- count in fives?
- count in odd numbers?
- count from 10 in twos?
- count backwards?

❧ Investigate the different ways that the calculator can count!

Name _____

Colour match

Colour match

You will need: some coloured rods.

❖ Find the 5 rod which is yellow.

❖ Using the other coloured rods, how many pairs of rods can you find to match the yellow 5 rod?

❖ Record your pairs with colours, like this:

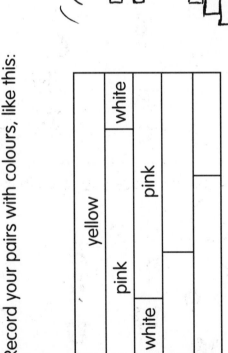

pink + white = yellow

❖ Now record them with numbers.
For example: 4 + 1 = 5

❖ Give each colour rod a symbol.
For example: pink = p, white = w, yellow = y.

❖ Record your pairs using symbols.
For example: p + w = y

❖ Now try using a 10 rod. Which pairs of rods will match the 10?

❖ Which combinations of three rods will match the 10? Record your combinations using your symbols.

❖ Investigate other rods.

Name _____

A-r-r-o-w-g-r-a-p-h-s ↗

✤ How many chains of numbers can you find in each arrowgraph by following the instruction given in the top left-hand corner? Use a different colour for each chain. One has been done to start you off.

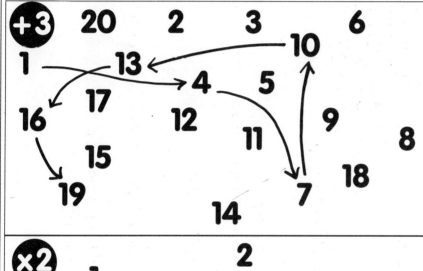

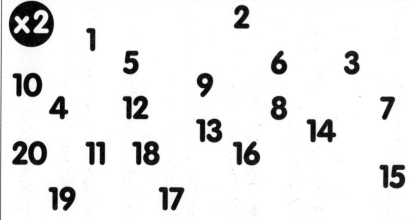

✤ Now choose your own instruction.

Function mazes

Function mazes

Here is a function maze.

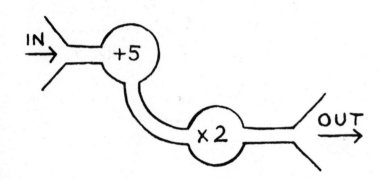

Feed in 2 and 14 comes out.

❖ What happens when these numbers go into this maze?

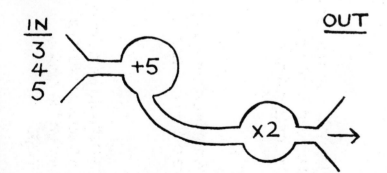

❖ Now try this maze.

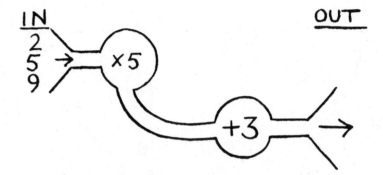

This maze has three functions.
❖ Try feeding in these numbers:

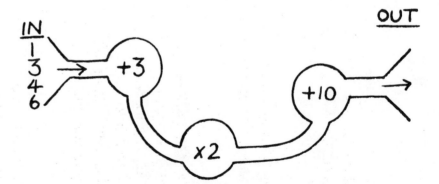

Make up some function mazes of your own and try them on a friend.

Magic dice

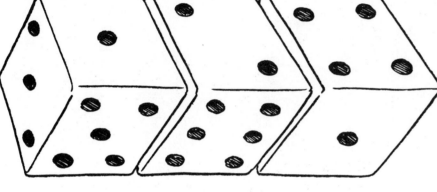

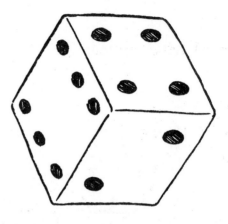

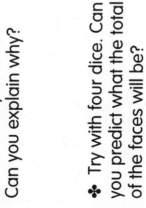

❧ Stack three dice so that a 3 shows on the top.

❧ Add the numbers on all the faces that you can see.

❧ Then let your partner restack the dice, again making sure that there is a 3 on top. Again add together the numbers on all the faces you can see.

❧ What do you notice? Can you explain why?

❧ Try with four dice. Can you predict what the total of the faces will be?

❧ What happens if you have a 6 on the top?

❧ Investigate other stacks of dice and record your results on the back of this page.

Picture value

Name _____

Picture value

❖ Can you work out what number each symbol is?

🌸 +	🌸 +	🌸 +	🌸	= 8	🌸	=
+	+	+	+			
🌸 +	🌸 +	🌳 +	🌳	= 10	🌳	=
+	+	+	+			
🌳 +	🚗 +	🏠 +	🌳	= 15	🚗	=
+	+	+	+			
🏠 +	🏠 +	🚗 +	🌸	= 16	🏠	=
12	13	14	?			

❖ What does the last column add up to?

Name _____

Table patterns

❖ Colour the multiples of 2.
❖ What do you notice?

1	2	3	4	5	6	7	8	9	10
11	12	13	14	15	16	17	18	19	20
21	22	23	24	25	26	27	28	29	30
31	32	33	34	35	36	37	38	39	40
41	42	43	44	45	46	47	48	49	50
51	52	53	54	55	56	57	58	59	60
61	62	63	64	65	66	67	68	69	70
71	72	73	74	75	76	77	78	79	80
81	82	83	84	85	86	87	88	89	90
91	92	93	94	95	96	97	98	99	100

❖ Colour the multiples of 4.
❖ Describe the pattern.

1	2	3	4	5	6	7	8	9	10
11	12	13	14	15	16	17	18	19	20
21	22	23	24	25	26	27	28	29	30
31	32	33	34	35	36	37	38	39	40
41	42	43	44	45	46	47	48	49	50
51	52	53	54	55	56	57	58	59	60
61	62	63	64	65	66	67	68	69	70
71	72	73	74	75	76	77	78	79	80
81	82	83	84	85	86	87	88	89	90
91	92	93	94	95	96	97	98	99	100

❖ Colour the multiples of 3.
❖ What pattern can you see?

1	2	3	4	5	6	7	8	9	10
11	12	13	14	15	16	17	18	19	20
21	22	23	24	25	26	27	28	29	30
31	32	33	34	35	36	37	38	39	40
41	42	43	44	45	46	47	48	49	50
51	52	53	54	55	56	57	58	59	60
61	62	63	64	65	66	67	68	69	70
71	72	73	74	75	76	77	78	79	80
81	82	83	84	85	86	87	88	89	90
91	92	93	94	95	96	97	98	99	100

❖ Colour the multiples of 5.
❖ Is this what you expected?

1	2	3	4	5	6	7	8	9	10
11	12	13	14	15	16	17	18	19	20
21	22	23	24	25	26	27	28	29	30
31	32	33	34	35	36	37	38	39	40
41	42	43	44	45	46	47	48	49	50
51	52	53	54	55	56	57	58	59	60
61	62	63	64	65	66	67	68	69	70
71	72	73	74	75	76	77	78	79	80
81	82	83	84	85	86	87	88	89	90
91	92	93	94	95	96	97	98	99	100

❖ Investigate other patterns of multiples.

Egyptian counting

Egyptian counting

The Ancient Egyptians used picture symbols to represent their numbers. Their picture symbols were called 'hieroglyphs'.

Single strokes were used for numbers up to 9 and then picture symbols were used for 10, 100, 1000, 10,000, 100,000 and 1,000,000.

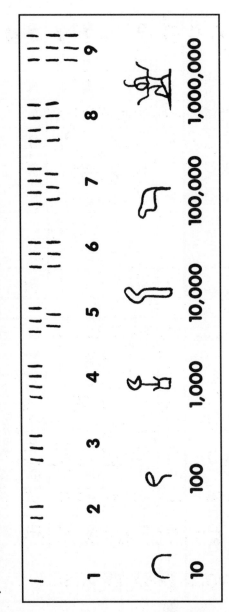

♣ Change these hierogryphs to our numerals:

1

2

3

4

♣ Change these numbers to Ancient Egyptian numerals:

1 47

2 216

3 549

4 3,715

5 72,409

6 224,370

• • • • • • • • • • • • **Crack the code** • • • • • • • • • • • •

This code is based on the position of dots in a grid.

A		D		G	
B		E		H	
C		F		I	
J		M		P	
K		N		Q	
L		O		R	
S		V		Y	
T		W		Z	
U		X			

So, O is written as:

J is written as:

V is written as:

✤ Decode the following messages:

1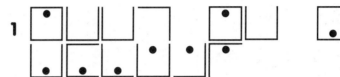

2

3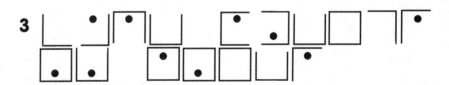

✤ Put these messages into code:

1 MAKE SURE YOU ARE NOT LATE

2 SEND YOUR REPLY BY POST

Consecutive numbers

—C-o-n-s-e-c-u-t-i-v-e- -n-u-m-b-e-r-s→

♣ Find the numbers between 1 and 50 which **cannot** be made
by adding consecutive numbers.

1	2	3	4	5	6	7	8	9	10
11	12	13	14	15	16	17	18	19	20
21	22	23	24	25	26	27	28	29	30
31	32	33	34	35	36	37	38	39	40
41	42	43	44	45	46	47	48	49	50

Here are some which
can be made:

$3 = 1 + 2$

$9 = 4 + 5$

$14 = 2 + 3 + 4 + 5$

$30 = 9 + 10 + 11$

$47 = 23 + 24$

♣ Circle the numbers which are left. Can you see a pattern here?

Name _____

Jumping frogs

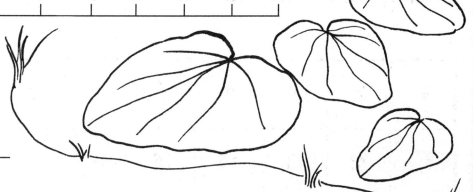

| 0 | 1 | 2 | 3 | 4 | 5 | 6 | 7 | 8 | 9 | 10 | 11 | 12 | 13 | 14 |

Imagine you own a frog that only jumps in a regular pattern. Today he is jumping a small jump followed by a larger jump (see above). He lands on the numbers:

$0 \rightarrow 2 \rightarrow 5 \rightarrow 7 \rightarrow 10 \rightarrow 12$

❖ What is the jumping rule? _____

❖ What are the next four numbers that your frog will land on?

_____

Sometimes your frog jumps differently.

❖ Find the rule and the next four numbers your frog will land on if it jumps in these sequences:

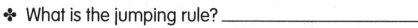
$0 \rightarrow 4 \rightarrow 7 \rightarrow 11 \rightarrow 14$ _____

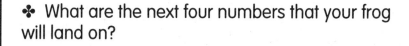
$0 \rightarrow 6 \rightarrow 9 \rightarrow 15 \rightarrow 18$ _____

$0 \rightarrow 7 \rightarrow 12 \rightarrow 19 \rightarrow 24$ _____

Your frog can also jump backwards.

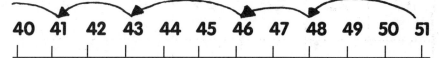

| 40 | 41 | 42 | 43 | 44 | 45 | 46 | 47 | 48 | 49 | 50 | 51 |

❖ What is the number sequence now?

_____

❖ Give the next four numbers.

_____

❖ Now make up your own rules for jumping frogs.

Name _____

Square-eyed

You will need: about 20 counters.

♣ The aim of this game is to cover with counters four numbers on the grid in a line, vertically, horizontally or diagonally.

♣ To cover a number, find the number from the circles which equals it. For example, for 169 on the grid you would choose 13^2.

♣ Record the number you select and the number you are aiming to cover up.

♣ You may have only one attempt at matching a circle with a grid square each turn. The first person to cover four connecting numbers is the winner.

♣ With your partner, check all the pairs of numbers you have used.

Square-eyed

225	121	169	900
784	49	441	81
289	1600	256	64
100	324	576	625

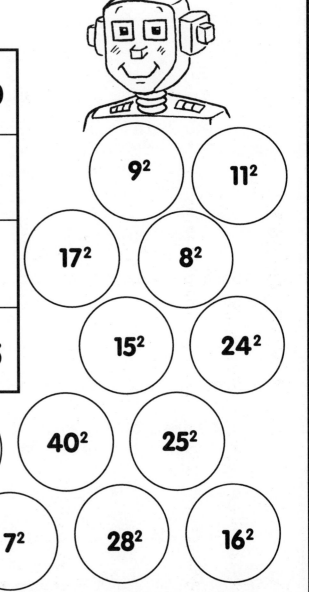

9^2 11^2

17^2 8^2

15^2 24^2

10^2 30^2 13^2 40^2 25^2

21^2 18^2 7^2 28^2 16^2

Name _____

Using letters

Remember $8 \times t$ can be written as **8t**.

❖ If $m = 10$, $n = 12$, $p = 6$ and $q = 5$, find the values of:

1 $3q + 4$

2 $m + 5p$

3 $12 + 3n$

4 $n - 2q$

5 $5q + m$

6 $\dfrac{pq}{m}$

7 $\dfrac{np}{6}$

8 $\dfrac{qn}{p}$

♣ Look at this number sentence:

$\square = \triangle + 4$

If $\triangle$ is worth 2, then $\square$ is worth 6.

♣ Now solve these:

1 If $\square = \triangle + 5$

What is the value of $\square$, if $\triangle = 3, 5, 7, 9$?

2 If $\triangle = \square - 2$

What is the value of $\square$, if $\triangle = 2, 4, 6, 8, 10$?

Name _____

Sequences

Sequences

Here is a sequence of numbers:

$3 \rightarrow 7 \rightarrow 11 \rightarrow 15 \rightarrow 19$
$\quad +4 \quad +4 \quad +4 \quad +4$

The numbers increase by 4 each time.

3   7   11   15   19

✤ Complete each of the following sequences for a total of eight terms altogether.

1	6	11	16	21	26	_____	_____	_____
2	72	65	58	51	44	_____	_____	_____
3	10	13	17	20	24	_____	_____	_____
4	60	55	53	48	46	_____	_____	_____
5	$\frac{3}{4}$	1	$1\frac{1}{4}$	$1\frac{1}{2}$	$1\frac{3}{4}$	_____	_____	_____
6	$2\frac{1}{2}$	$3\frac{1}{2}$	$4\frac{1}{2}$	$5\frac{1}{2}$	$6\frac{1}{2}$	_____	_____	_____
7	18	$17\frac{1}{4}$	$16\frac{1}{2}$	$15\frac{3}{4}$	15	_____	_____	_____
8	$\frac{5}{10}$	$\frac{7}{10}$	$1\frac{1}{10}$	$1\frac{3}{10}$	$1\frac{7}{10}$	_____	_____	_____
9	1.0	1.2	1.4	1.6	1.8	_____	_____	_____
10	20.3	19.8	19.3	18.8	18.3	_____	_____	_____
11	18.5	18.25	18.0	17.75	17.5	_____	_____	_____
12	1.32	1.44	1.56	1.68	1.8	_____	_____	_____

Teacher Timesavers: Maths puzzles

Name _____

Which key?

You will need: a calculator.
In the number sentence below, the function keys are blank.

9 ☐ 3 ☐ 5 = 32

✤ Which two keys have to be pressed to give the right answer?

Here is the solution:

9 ☒ 3 ⊞ 5 = 32

✤ In each of these number sentences, insert the function keys needed (+, −, ×, ÷) and then check your answers on the calculator.

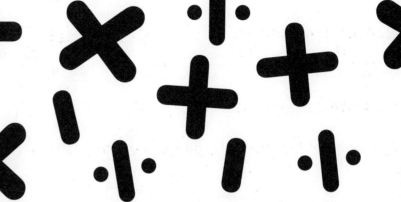

#						
1	5	☐	3	☐	4	= 32
2	6	☐	5	☐	7	= 7
3	8	☐	2	☐	2	= 5
4	10	☐	4	☐	8	= 14
5	5	☐	4	☐	2	= 10
6	20	☐	13	☐	3	= 21
7	30	☐	6	☐	19	= 24
8	56	☐	7	☐	4	= 4
9	9	☐	7	☐	20	= 43
10	70	☐	18	☐	2	= 26
11	96	☐	12	☐	8	= 64
12	100	☐	25	☐	3	= 25

Three jumps to 100

Three jumps to 100

✤ In this activity, you must use three jumps to reach 100. You may start at any number from 1 to 100 and you may use any of these signs: +, −, ÷, ×. For example:

$$\boxed{10} \xrightarrow{\times 9} \boxed{90} \xrightarrow{+ 7} \boxed{97} \xrightarrow{+ 3} \boxed{100}$$

You may only use a single digit for the operation. No two-digit numbers are allowed.

✤ Try to find a way to make 100 for every starting number from 1 to 100.

✤ What patterns do you notice?

1	2	3	4	5	6	7	8	9	10
11	12	13	14	15	16	17	18	19	20
21	22	23	24	25	26	27	28	29	30
31	32	33	34	35	36	37	38	39	40
41	42	43	44	45	46	47	48	49	50
51	52	53	54	55	56	57	58	59	60
61	62	63	64	65	66	67	68	69	70
71	72	73	74	75	76	77	78	79	80
81	82	83	84	85	86	87	88	89	90
91	92	93	94	95	96	97	98	99	100

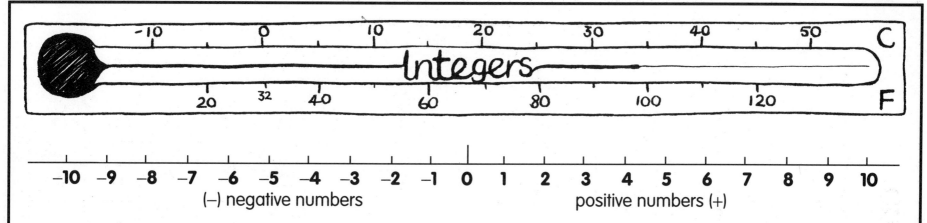

(−) negative numbers   positive numbers (+)

This is an integer number line. Numbers on the right-hand side of the line are positive (+) numbers. Numbers on the left-hand side of the line are negative (−) numbers.

If you start at −3 and jump four spaces in a positive direction you land on +1. If you start on +2 and jump six spaces in a negative direction you land on −4.

♣ Use the integer number line to help you to solve these problems.

1 Start at −5 and jump eight spaces in a positive direction. Where do you land?

2 Start at +3 and jump six spaces in a negative direction. Where do you land?

3 Moving in a positive direction, complete this number sequence: −8, −5, −2, _____ , _____ , _____ .

Positive and negative numbers are used on a Celsius thermometer scale to show temperatures above and below freezing point (0°C).

♣ Use a thermometer to help you to work out these temperature problems.

4 By how many degrees has the temperature risen, if the 9 am reading is −3°C and the 2 pm reading is 4°C?

5 By how many degrees has the temperature fallen, if the 9 am reading is 2°C and the 2 pm reading is −6°C?

6 Find the average of these daily temperatures taken during December: 3°C, −2°C, 2°C, 5°C.

♣ Now use the number line to make up some similar sums of your own for a friend to try.

Name _____

Fibonacci

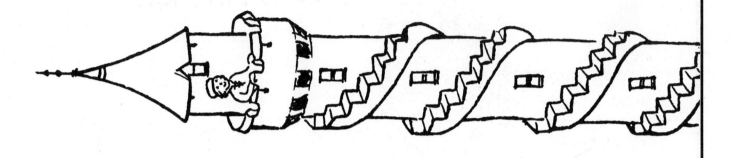

Fibonacci

Almost 800 years ago, an Italian called Leonardo Fibonacci created the number sequence shown in the box opposite. Each number is made by adding the two numbers which come before.

✤ Keep on adding numbers to the Fibonacci sequence.

✤ Now put a line under any number in the sequence. The total of all the numbers above the line is equal to one less than the second number below the line. Try this a few times.

✤ Here is another activity.
• Take any three numbers in the sequence.
• Multiply the middle number by itself. Then multiply the first and third numbers together.
• Try this a number of times. Do the answers have something in common?

0
1
1
2
3
5
8
13
21
34
55
89

Pascal's triangle

A pattern of numbers is used to make the triangle opposite. It is named after a seventeenth century French mathematician, called Blaise Pascal.

```
            1            = 1

         1     1         = 2

      1     2     1

   1     3     3     1

1     4     6     4     1
```

❖ Work out how the triangle is made. Then continue to make the lines so the triangle grows in size.

❖ Add the numbers **across** each line. Find a pattern in these numbers.

❖ Look for other patterns in the triangle's structure.

Name _____

Triangular patterns

Triangular patterns

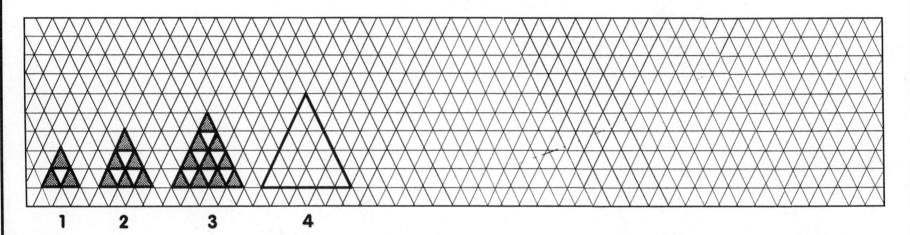

✤ Continue this pattern by shading in the correct number of small triangles in the large blank shape.

✤ Carry on the process by drawing the triangles yourself, following the same pattern of shading.

✤ Now complete the table opposite.

✤ Look down the columns. Investigate any number patterns you can see.

Shape	Total number of triangles	Shaded triangles	Unshaded
1	4	3	1
2	9	6	3
3			
4			
5			
6			
7			

Teacher Timesavers: Maths puzzles

Animal ears

♣ Draw big, curved ears on the elephant.

♣ Draw small, pointed ears on the cat.

♣ Draw very small, round ears on the mouse.

♣ Draw long, pointed ears on the rabbit.

Name _____

Animal magic

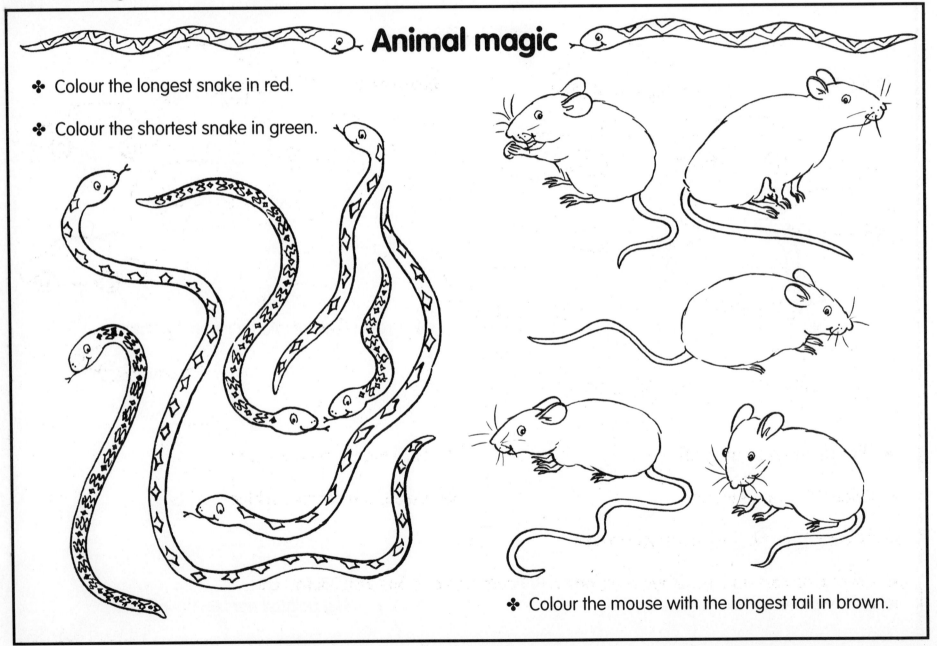

Animal magic

❖ Colour the longest snake in red.

❖ Colour the shortest snake in green.

❖ Colour the mouse with the longest tail in brown.

Car chase

Paul's cars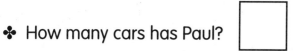

Laura's cars

❖ How many cars has Paul? ☐

❖ Colour Paul's cars in red.

❖ Who could make the longest line of cars?

❖ Cut out the cars and make two lines, one with Paul's cars and one with Laura's cars, to see if you are right.

❖ How many cars has Laura? ☐

❖ Colour Laura's cars in blue.

Repeating shapes

Name _____

Repeating shapes

✤ Continue these patterns:

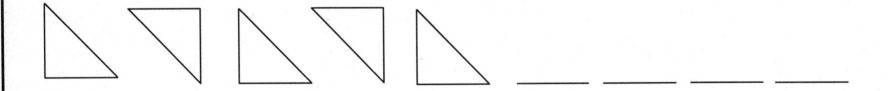

✤ Make some patterns of your own with shapes like these:

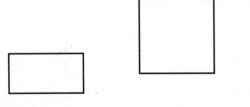

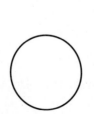
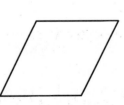

Name _____

B l o c k   p a t t e r n s

You will need: some blocks.

♣ Copy and continue these patterns with blocks:

♣ Make some patterns of your own with blocks.

♣ Draw them on the back of this page.

Name _____

Colour spots

Colour spots

You will need: some coloured counters.

✤ Use red and yellow counters to make this pattern:

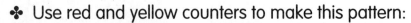

✤ Now copy this pattern:

✤ Use two sets of counters, each of a different colour, to make your own pattern.

✤ Copy your pattern here:

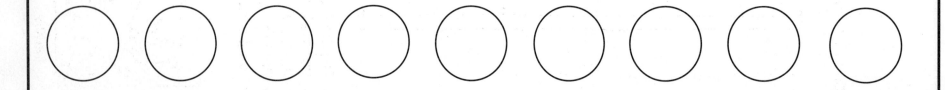

Name _____

Tidy the toy cupboard

Can you help to put the toys away?

❖ Put the teddy on the bottom shelf.
❖ Put the ball on the top shelf.
❖ Put the bat next to the ball.
❖ Put the book above the teddy.
❖ Put the clock on the middle shelf.

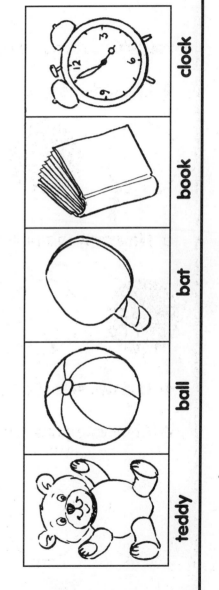

teddy   ball   bat   book   clock

Teacher Timesavers: Maths puzzles

75

Name _____

Robo-shape

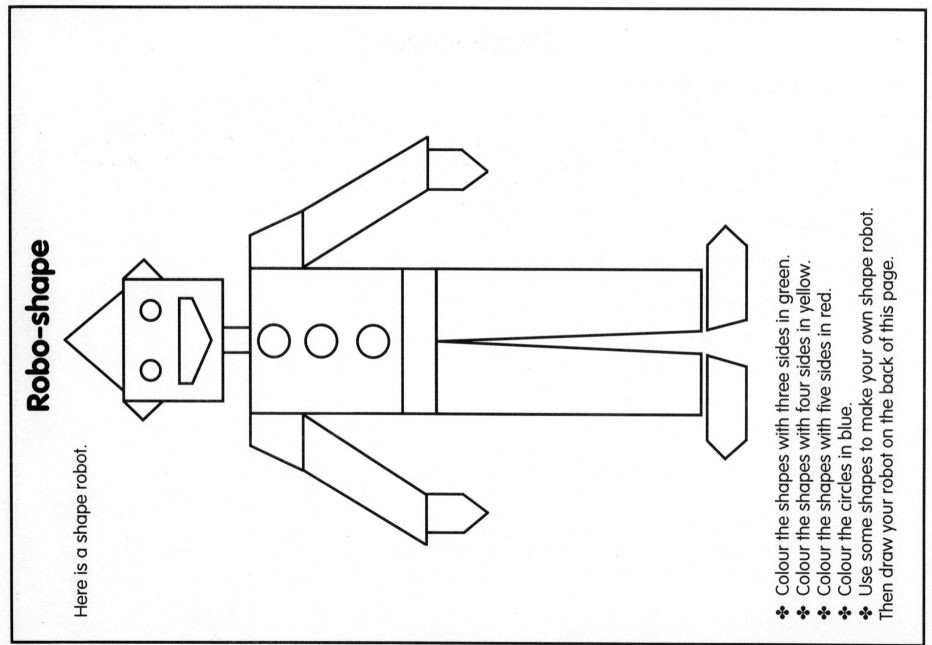

Robo-shape

Here is a shape robot.

❖ Colour the shapes with three sides in green.
❖ Colour the shapes with four sides in yellow.
❖ Colour the shapes with five sides in red.
❖ Colour the circles in blue.
❖ Use some shapes to make your own shape robot.
Then draw your robot on the back of this page.

Shape snake

Here is a snake made from shapes.

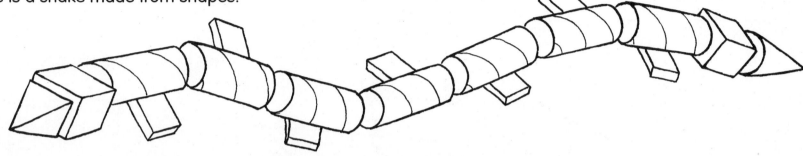

✤ Find some shapes like these and make your own snake shape.

✤ Draw your shape snake here.

Name _____

Shipshapes

 Shipshapes

Here are a square and two right-angled triangles.

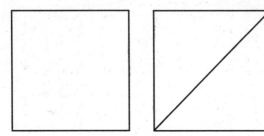

✤ Find some shapes like these, or cut them out of card.

This is one shape picture that you can make with them:

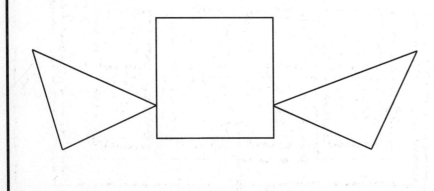

✤ What other shapes can you make?

✤ What shapes can you make when you can only match together edges that are the same length? Here is one:

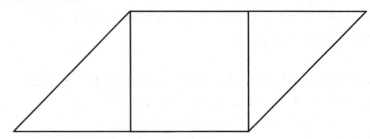

- How many can you make?
- Can you name the shapes you make?
- Can you describe them?

Metre maze

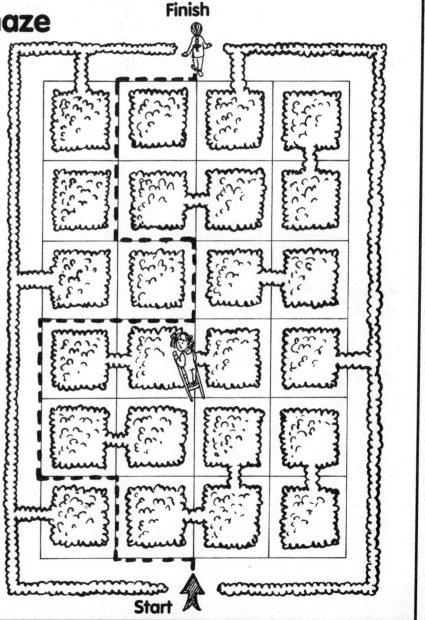

This maze is marked in metre sections.

Leela's route is shown, she turned through ten right angles and walked 12 metres.

✤ Find another route that turns through ten right angles. How long is it?

✤ Find the shortest route. How many right-angle turns are there? How long is this route?

✤ Now find the longest route. How long is it? How many right-angle turns are there in it?

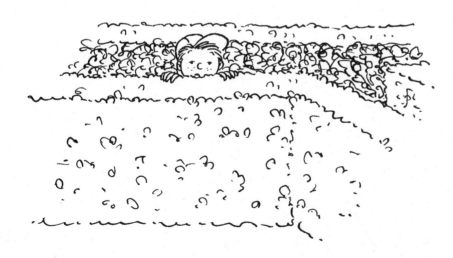

Name _____

 # Jack-in-the-box

✤ Cut out this shape and fold it to make a box.

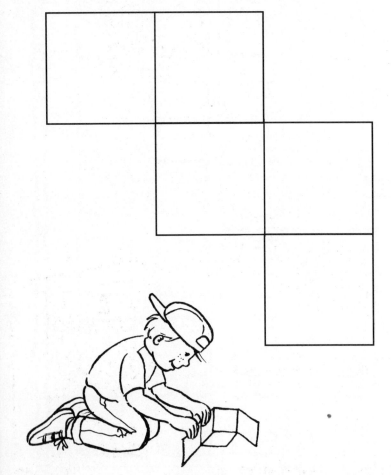

✤ Where could you have added another square, before cutting it out, to make a box with a lid?

✤ Draw your net.

✤ Investigate! Find as many nets as you can that will make a box with a lid. You may need squared paper for this activity.

Shopping shapes

You will need: some solid shapes and some empty boxes and containers.

Here are some items from a shopping bag.

_____

_____

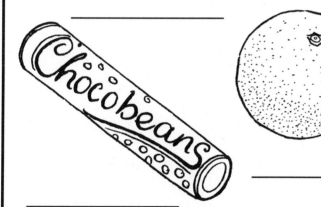

_____

_____

♣ Find a solid shape to match each item.
❀ Write the name of the shape underneath each item.
♣ What other shapes can you find to match things which may be in a shopping bag?
❀ Make a collection of different-shaped packages.

_____

Riddle-me-shape

Riddle-me-shape

✤ Try to solve these shape riddles.

I am a flat shape.
I have four sides and four right angles.
All my sides are the same length.
What am I?

_____

I am a flat shape.
I have five sides.
I have five angles.
What am I?

_____

I am a solid shape.
I have no flat faces.
I have no edges.
What am I?

_____

I am a solid shape.
I have 24 right angles.
I have six faces.
All my edges are the same length.
What am I?

_____

✤ Make up some shape riddles of your own. Give
them to a friend to work out.

Shape pictures

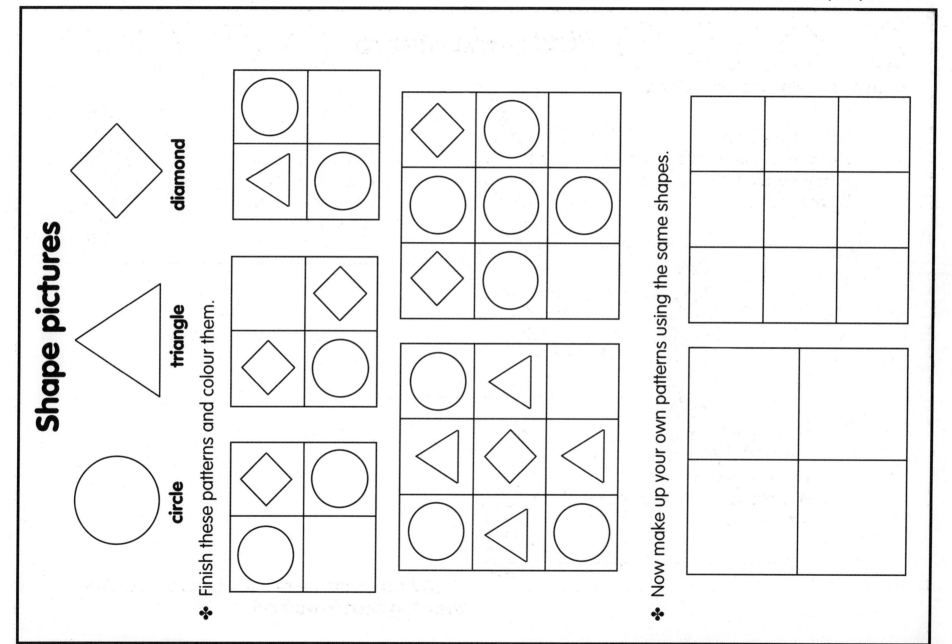

◇ diamond

△ triangle

○ circle

♣ Finish these patterns and colour them.

♣ Now make up your own patterns using the same shapes.

Name _____

Halving

Halving

You want to share a chocolate bar with a friend.

❖ What about a square chocolate bar?

❖ In how many ways can you halve it?

Here are two ways of cutting it in half.

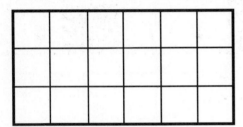

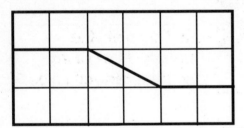

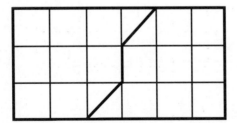

❖ Use squared paper to find out how many ways you can halve the chocolate.

❖ Investigate the ways in which you can divide a square into two equal parts.

Name _____

P	a	t	t	e	r	n

s	q	u	a	r	e	s

❖ Copy this patterned square on to squared paper. Colour all the shaded squares using one colour.

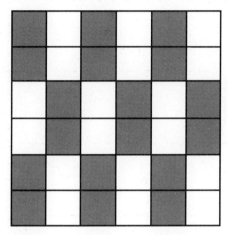

❖ How many squares are coloured?

❖ Copy and complete this pattern.

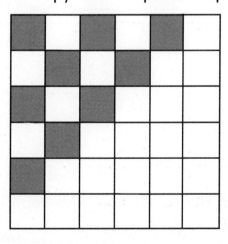

❖ How many squares are coloured?

❖ Copy the pattern below.

❖ First, how many squares do you **think** will be coloured when the pattern is complete?

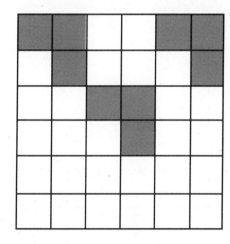

❖ Complete the pattern. How many squares did you colour?

❖ Use the same-sized square and make up some patterns of your own, using just one colour.

My day

Name _____

My day

❧ This is Jill's day. Complete the clocks.

Get up	School starts	Lunchtime	Hometime	Teatime	Bedtime
7:30	**8:50**	**12:00**	**15:15**	**:**	**20:00**

  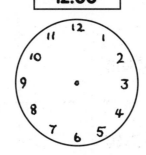   

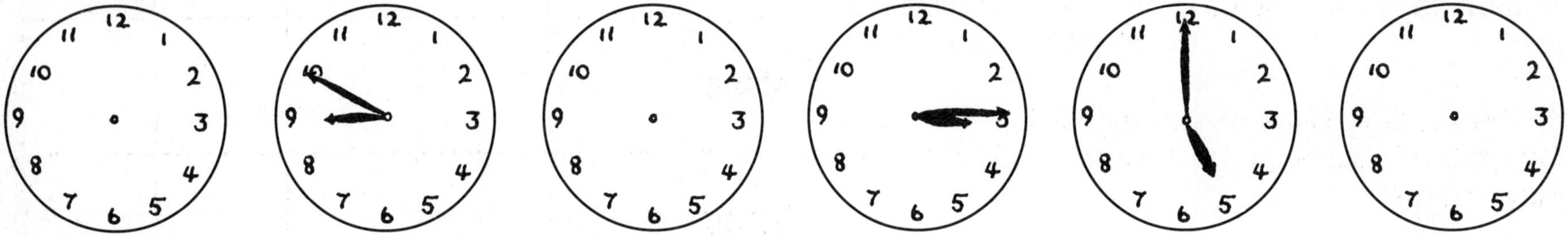

seven thirty _____ _____ _____ five o'clock _____

❧ Fill in the times for your day.

:	:	:	:	:	:

 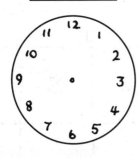 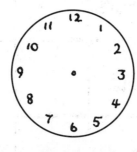 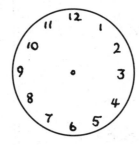  (sixth blank clock)

_____ _____ _____ _____ _____ _____

Calendar puzzle

Some numbers have been missed off the May page of this calendar.

✤ Fill in the missing dates.

✤ The last day of May was a Wednesday. Can you work out what day the first day of May was on?

_____

✤ On this calendar, how many Saturdays were there in May?

_____

✤ How many Saturdays will there be on this calendar in June?

_____

✤ Think of some questions you could ask a friend about this calendar. Write them on the back of the sheet.

May					
Sun					
Mon					
Tues					
Wed					**31**
Thurs					
Fri			**19**		
Sat					

Name _____

Compass points

✤ Use a ruler to join the marked points.

✤ From START:

- go W   5 cm;

- go NE   7 cm;

- go S   9 cm;

- go W   7 cm;

- go SE   4 cm;

- go E   11 cm;

- go NE   4 cm;

- go W   10 cm;

- go N   2 cm;

- go E   10 cm;

- go NW 14 cm;

- go S   8 cm.

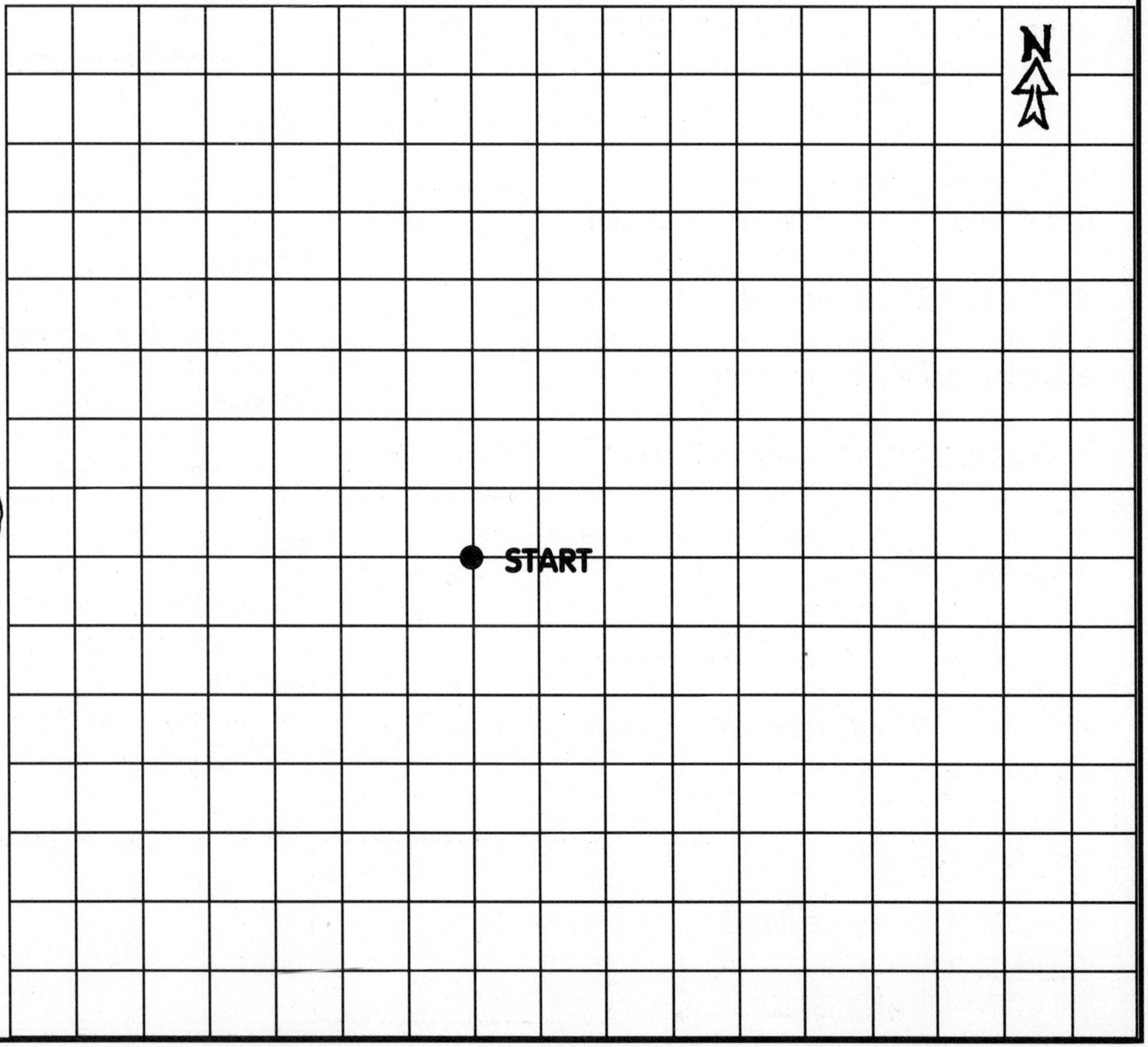

Compass points

● START

Name _____

Shapes in pieces

This shape: is a half of this:

This shape: is a quarter of this:

✤ Look carefully at the shapes below.

✤ Match the whole shape with its half and its quarter.

Here is a square.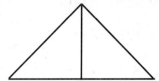

If we cut it in half along the dotted line, these are some of the shapes we can make with the pieces.

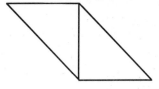

✤ Cut out the triangle at the bottom of the page and stick it on to card and cut it in half.

✤ Draw the different shapes you can make with the pieces.

✤ Investigate halves and quarters of other shapes.

Name _____

Mirror pictures

Mirror pictures

✦ Complete these drawings and colour them.

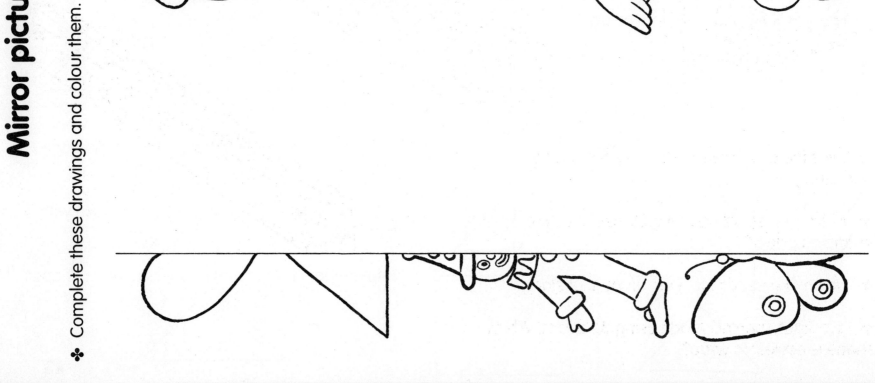

Name _____

   **Birthday presents**

Here are three parcels the size of eight cubes fixed together.

Each parcel is wrapped with paper and tied with string.

✤ Investigate with real cubes, old newspaper and string.

✤ Which parcel will need the biggest piece of wrapping paper?

✤ Which one needs the least amount of string?

✤ Investigate parcels made using 36 cubes. Which shape is easiest to wrap?

Name _____

Big hand

  **Big hand**

♣ Draw around your hand in the space below.

♣ Estimate how many counters will be needed to cover your hand shape. ☐

♣ Cover your hand shape with counters.
♣ How many were needed? ☐

♣ Estimate how many Multilink cubes will cover your hand shape. ☐

♣ Cover your hand shape with Multilink cubes.
♣ How many were needed? ☐

♣ Estimate how many centicubes will cover your hand shape. ☐

♣ Cover your hand with centicubes.
♣ How many were needed? ☐

♣ Use some other materials to work out the area of your handshape.

♣ Compare your results with your friends'. Which are the best units to use to measure area?

Name _____

Multi squares

♣ Choose two points. Join them and then draw three more lines to complete a square. Like this:

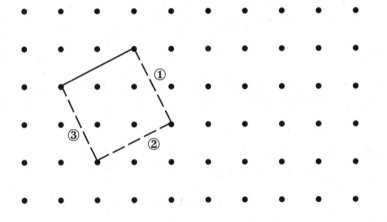

♣ Investigate how many squares you could draw on the grid below. You could use a 5 × 5 nailboard to try out your ideas first. There are more than you think!

♣ Choose another two points. Join them and complete the square.

What comes next?

What comes next?

♣ What will the next shape look like in each group?

♣ Continue the sequences of shapes.

Squares

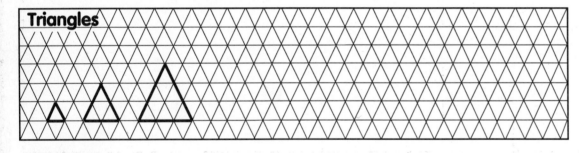

♣ Look at the areas and perimeters of the sequences for any patterns which might be produced.

For example: the squares have areas of 1, 4, 9... and perimeters of 4, 8, 12....

♣ Look at similar sequences made using hexagons or other shapes.

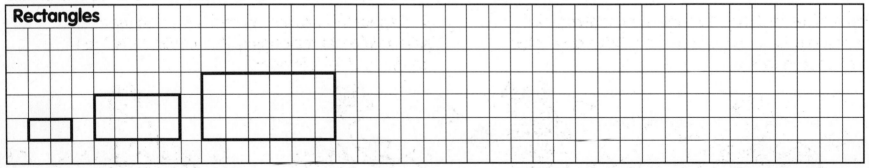

Tiling

❖ Cut out some small square tiles.

❖ What is the smallest number of tiles which would be required to make four different rectangles of the same area? Investigate and make more tiles when you need them.

Draw your four rectangles here:

Remember that the rectangles must always be completely filled in and must not have any holes or spaces in them.

❖ What is the smallest number of tiles needed to make five different rectangles of the same area?

Draw your five rectangles here:

❖ Repeat this process to make six and then seven different rectangles. You could draw them on the back of this page.

Pentominoes

Pentominoes

These shapes are called pentominoes. They have an area of five squares.

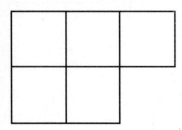

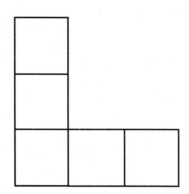

♣ Find the rest of the pentomino family. There are ten more ways in which you can arrange five squares.

♣ Try these activities with your pentominoes. You may use them any way round and with either face uppermost.

• Take some of the pentominoes and make them into rectangles.

For example:

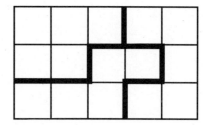

• Take some of the pentominoes and make them into steps.

For example:

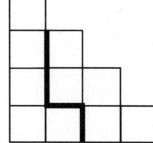

• Draw a rectangular grid ten squares by six squares. Now fit all your pentominoes into this rectangle. There are several solutions!

Upside-down

❧ Arrange some pennies like this:

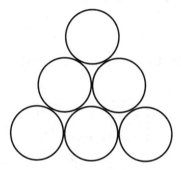

❧ What is the smallest number of moves you need to make to turn this shape upside-down?

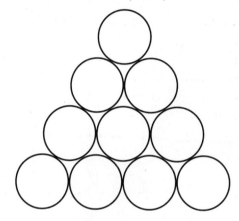

❧ Now turn the shape upside down **by moving only two pennies** to look like this:

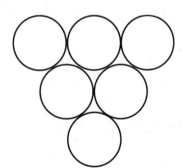

Fraction grids

Fraction grids

These $\frac{1}{2}$ and $\frac{1}{2}$ patterns ($\frac{1}{2}$ coloured and $\frac{1}{2}$ uncoloured) have been made on a 4 × 4 grid.

♣ Using the same grid system, make some $\frac{1}{2}$ and $\frac{1}{2}$ patterns of your own.

♣ Now use a 4 × 4 grid and make some $\frac{1}{4}$ and $\frac{3}{4}$ patterns and some $\frac{3}{8}$ and $\frac{5}{8}$ patterns.

♣ Are there other fraction patterns you can make using the same grid?

Name _____

Nets

This net will fold up to make a cube.

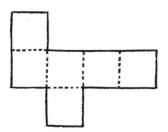 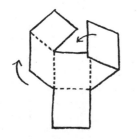

♣ Here are some more nets. Which ones will make cubes?

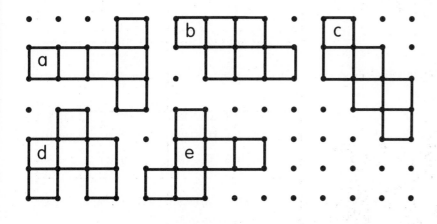

♣ Try to find all the possible nets of a cube.

♣ How many different nets are there for a tetrahedron? Try drawing them below.

Name _____

Sizing up

Sizing up

Five thousand years ago, in Ancient Egypt, people used their hands and bodies for measuring:

A digit – width of the first finger at the knuckle.

A palm – distance across the palm counting the thumb.

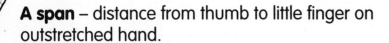

A span – distance from thumb to little finger on outstretched hand.

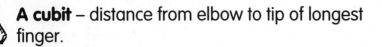

A cubit – distance from elbow to tip of longest finger.

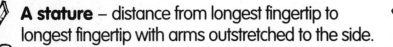

A stature – distance from longest fingertip to longest fingertip with arms outstretched to the side.

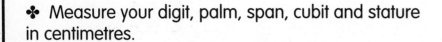

❖ Measure your digit, palm, span, cubit and stature in centimetres.

❖ Record your results below.

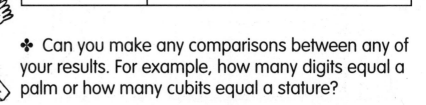

❖ Can you make any comparisons between any of your results. For example, how many digits equal a palm or how many cubits equal a stature?

❖ Try the same measurements from some of your friends. How do they compare?

❖ Can the same comparisons be made with similar measurements taken from adults?

100

Name _____

Tangrams

This activity is based on the ancient Chinese game of 'tangrams'.
The shapes are drawn on to a grid of 2cm squares.

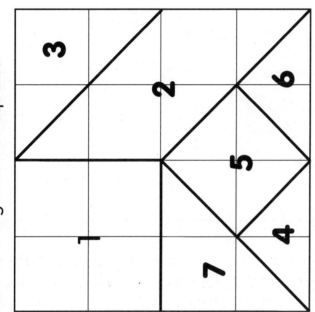

✽ First, fill in this table.

Shape number	Name of shape	Area of shape (cm²)
1		
2		
3		
4		
5		
6		
7		

✽ Cut out the shapes. Fit them together, by touching but **not** overlapping.
You should be able to make the following:
- a square with two shapes;
- a rectangle with three shapes;
- a square with three shapes;
- a rectangle with four shapes;
- a triangle with four shapes.

✽ Use the pieces to make new shapes of your own.

Three in a row

Three in a row

This 3 × 3 square has three circles in a line.

♣ How many circles could you put on a 3 × 3 grid **without** getting three in a line?

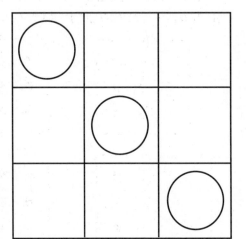

This 4 × 4 square also has three circles in a line.

♣ How many circles could you put on a 4 × 4 grid **without** getting three in a line?

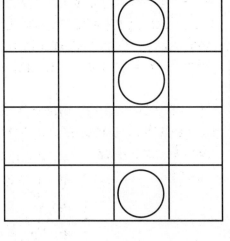

♣ Repeat the process with a 5 × 5 square and then a 6 × 6 square and so on.

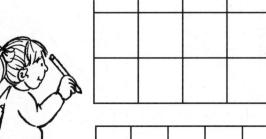

Reflections

You will need: a 3 × 3 nailboard, some elastic bands, 'dotty' paper and a pencil.

❖ Using your 3 × 3 nailboard and the elastic bands, make the following shapes with the dotted line shown below as a line of symmetry:

- an isosceles triangle;
- a pentagon;
- a kite.

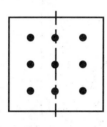

❖ Draw the shapes on to 'dotty' paper.

❖ Repeat the same shapes as above, but with this new line of symmetry:

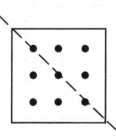

❖ Again draw the shapes on 'dotty' paper.

❖ Place elastic bands on to the nailboards as shown in the diagrams below.

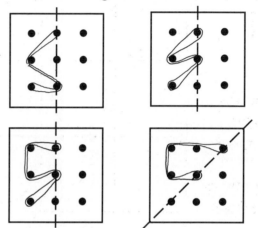

❖ If the dotted line on each diagram is a line of symmetry, place a second band on the nailboard to make the other half of each symmetrical design. Record the patterns on 'dotty' paper.

❖ This symmetrical design is made by overlapping two elastic bands. Make up some designs of your own in this way.

Get the point

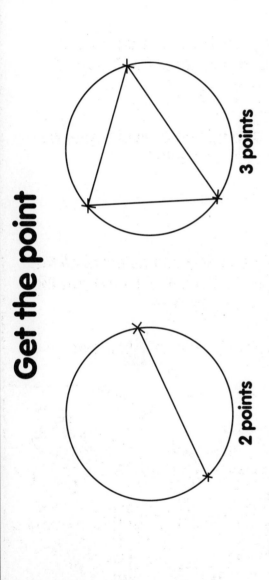

3 points

2 points

❖ Fill in this table for the two circles shown above. Can you predict the answers for 4, 5 and then 6 points on the circle?

Number of points on circle	2	3	4	5	6
Estimate of number of parts of circle					
Actual number of parts of circle					

❖ Complete these diagrams to check your answers. Write the actual number of parts of the circle into the table.

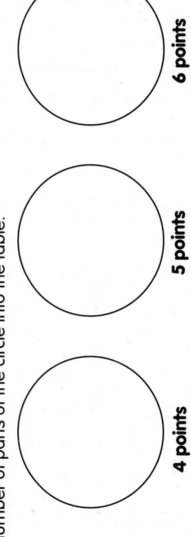

4 points

5 points

6 points

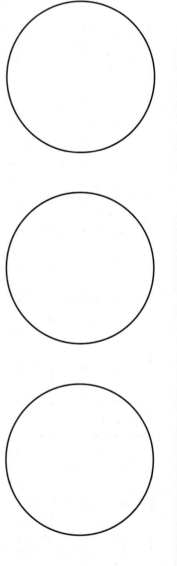

❖ What answers would you get for 7 points, 8 points and so on? Is there a pattern in the answers to help you make the predictions? Investigate using these circles and draw more on the back of this page if you need them.

Fences

Name _____

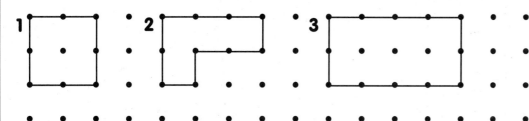

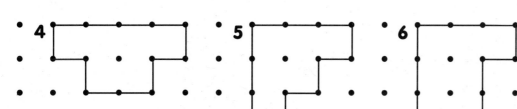

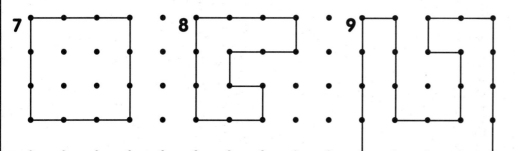

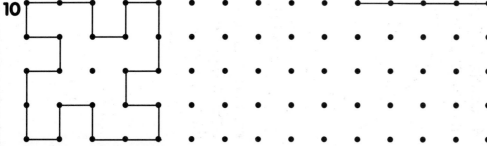

The 'fence' gives this shape an area of 3 squares and a perimeter of 8 units.

1 unit

This shape also has an area of 3 squares and a perimeter of 8 units.

✿ Find the areas and perimeters of all the shapes opposite. Do any of them have the same area and perimeter?

✿ Use dotty paper to make your own 'fence' shapes.

Circle surprise

Circle surprise

circumference

diameter

♣ Make a collection of circular objects.

♣ Measure the diameter and the circumference of each circle to the nearest $\frac{1}{2}$ cm and enter your measurements into the table below. To measure the circumference of each object, you will have to use a piece of cotton or thin string.

Object	Diameter (D)	Circumference (C)	C ÷ D

♣ What do you notice about your results?

♣ What is the ratio of the circumference to the diameter, to the nearest whole number?

Name _____

Plotting points

❖ On the grid system below, plot these points in each
of the four quadrants: (2,2) (6,0) (6,5) (3,7) (1,5) (2,2).

❖ Join the points in order.

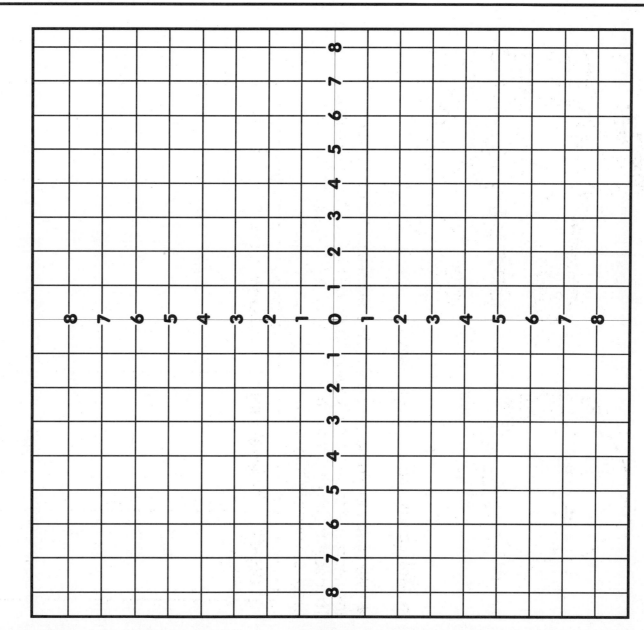

❖ What shapes have you made?

❖ Are all the shapes the same?

Name _____

Find your way

Find your way

* Use a protractor and ruler to find the bearings and distances from P to U.

* Repeat the process from U back to P.

Scale 1cm : 1km

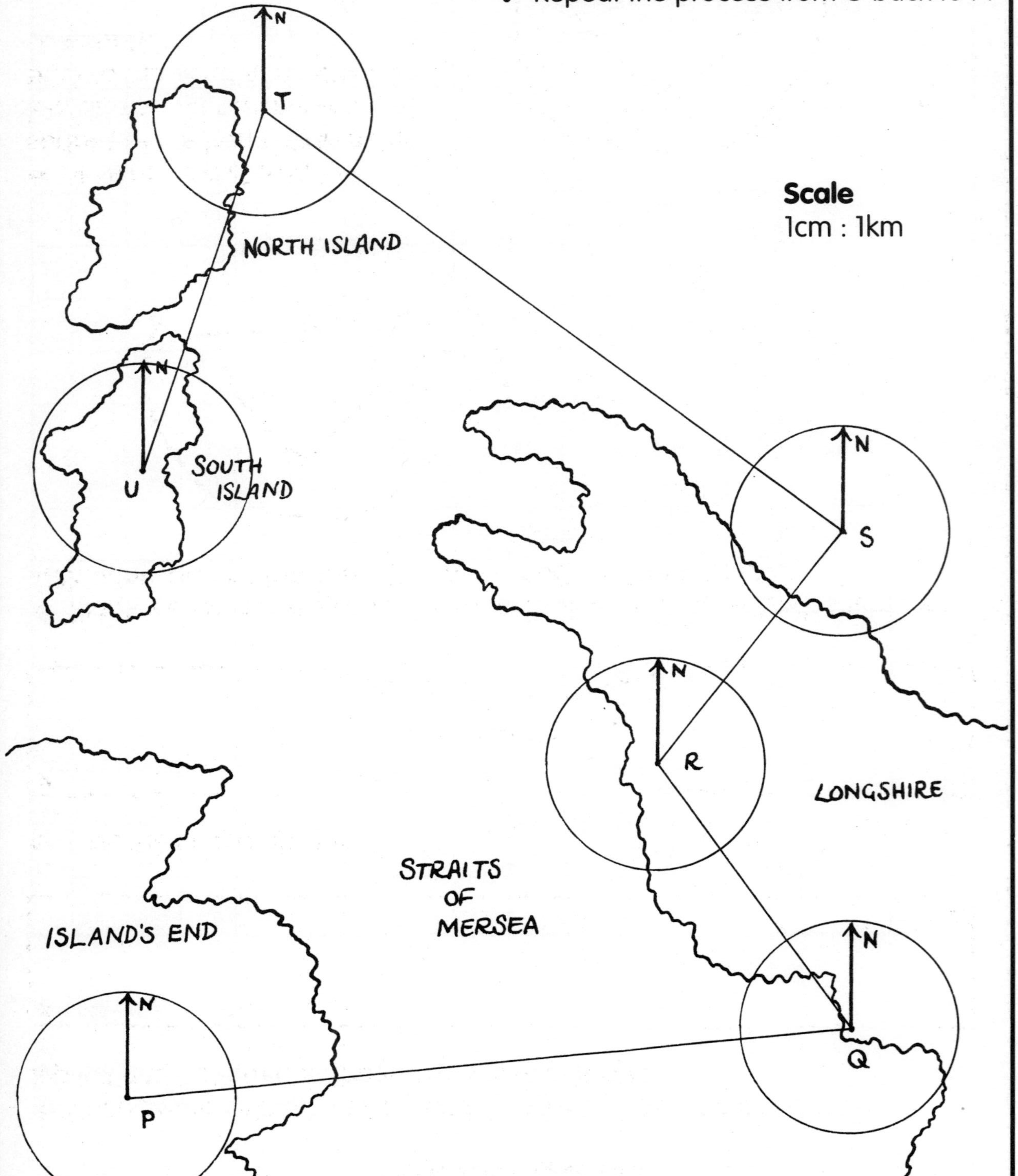

LONGSHIRE

STRAITS OF MERSEA

NORTH ISLAND

SOUTH ISLAND

ISLAND'S END

S

R

Q

T

U

P

Name _____

Möbius band

✤ Cut a paper strip 30cm long and 5cm wide. Place a cross in the top left and bottom right-hand corners of one side.

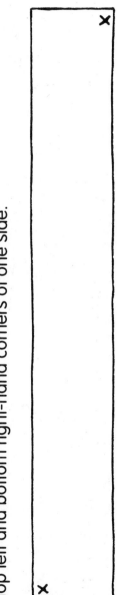

✤ Give the strip a half turn.

✤ Place the two crosses on top of one another and fix the ends together with adhesive or sticky tape. You have made a 'Möbius band'.

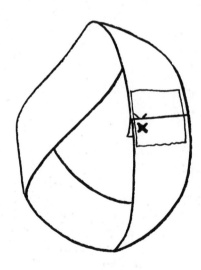

✤ Now draw a line on the surface of the band. Start at the join and go round until you get back to the beginning. What do you notice?

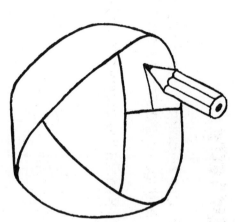

✤ Colour in one surface of your band. What do you notice now?

Making two-dimensional shapes

You will need: a 5 × 5 nailboard, some elastic bands, 'dotty' paper and a pencil.

✤ Using the nailboard and elastic bands, make the following shapes:
- right-angled triangles;
- acute-angled triangles;
- obtuse-angled triangles;
- isosceles triangles;
- scalene triangles.

✤ Record your results on 'dotty' paper.

✤ Which triangles are right-angled **and** isosceles?

✤ Can you make an equilateral triangle?

✤ Make three different squares.

✤ Now make the following quadrilaterals:
- two different types of kite;
- two different parallelograms;
- two different trapeziums.

✤ Again record all your results on 'dotty' paper.

Towers of Hanoi

According to an ancient Buddhist story, a giant version of this problem, made with 100 different-sized golden disks arranged on poles, is the unending task of the priests of Hanoi.

You will need to make a playing board like this:

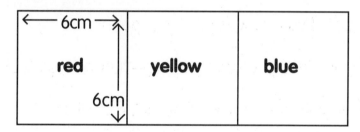

Also, you will need three card discs about $2\frac{1}{2}$ cm, 2cm and $1\frac{1}{2}$ cm in radius.

✤ Stack the discs in order of size on the red section. The smallest disc should be on the top.

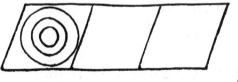

✤ The purpose of the game is to move the three discs on to the blue section, still in size order.

✤ You **must** follow these rules:
• large discs cannot be placed on smaller ones;
• you can move only one disc at a time;
• you can only move the top disc in any pile;
• you can place any disc in any of the sections;
• you cannot place discs side by side in the same section, only on top of each other.

✤ How many moves did it take you?

✤ What is the least number of moves needed to move the discs from the red to the blue square?

✤ Play the game again, but moving from the red to the yellow square.

Name _____

Circles in space

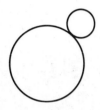

Circles in space

Using two different-sized circles, how many ways are there of positioning them in space?

Using the key opposite, this diagram showing three circles can be described as: I.I.L.

Shown below are five different ways of positioning the two circles:

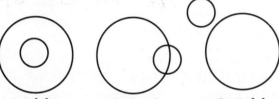

Inside   **Linked**   **Outside**

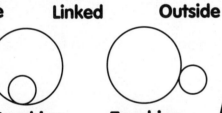

Touching (inside)   **Touching (outside)**

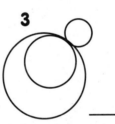

Key:
I   Inside
L   Linked
O   Outside
Ti   Touching (inside)
To   Touching (outside)

❖ Now describe these shapes using the key:

1
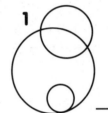

2
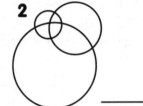
_____

3

4

_____

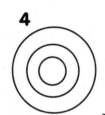

❖ Draw the following arrangements of circles on the back of this sheet. You may find that there is more than one way of doing them.

1 O.I.L.   **2** L.O.O.   **3** To.O.L.

Teacher Timesavers: Maths puzzles

Name _____

Big numbers

✤ Here are some timely problems. Use your calculator to help you.

> **Remember** There are 365 days in a year, but every fourth year there is a leap year with 366 days.

1983 1984 1985 1986 1987 1988 1989 1990 1991 1992 1993 1994 1995

After each answer, show how you used your calculator with a flow diagram. Use the back of this page if you need more room.

- If today is your 11th birthday, how many days have you lived?

- Work out your real age in days.

- Work out the ages in days of two of your friends.

Remember the leap years

Shoe muddle

Shoe muddle!

✤ Can you find the pairs?

✤ Join them with a line and colour them to match.

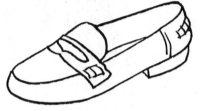

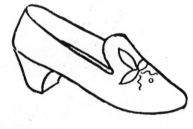

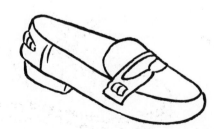

Name _____

Matching up

✤ Which of these objects usually go together?

✤ Draw a line to match up the partners; for example, cup and saucer.

Which set?

Name _____

Which set?

❖ Cut out the pictures at the bottom of the page and sort them into two sets.

❖ Explain how you have sorted the pictures.

_____

Name _____

What next?

❖ Look carefully at the two pictures below.

❖ For each picture, draw what you think will happen next.

❖ Draw your pictures here.

Birthday map

 # Birthday map

The children in 'Badger group' have mapped their birthdays on to a chart.

Badger group's birthdays

Ahmed	January
Ben	February
Claire	March
David	April
Emma	May
	June
	July
	August
	September
	October
	November
	December

✤ Working in groups of five or six children, write down the names of the children in your group and map their birthdays.

My group's birthdays

_____   January
_____   February
_____   March
_____   April
_____   May
_____   June
_____   July
_____   August
_____   September
_____   October
_____   November
_____   December

Name _____

Flaming June

Class 3 kept a record of the weather in June and recorded it using these symbols:

sunny   **rainy**   **cloudy**

Here is their weather chart:

Sunday		6	13	20	27
Monday		7	14	21	28
Tuesday	1	8	15	22	29
Wednesday	2	9	16	23	30
Thursday	3	10	17	24	
Friday	4	11	18	25	
Saturday	5	12	19	26	

✤ From Class 3's weather chart, count the number of:

- sunny days _____

- cloudy days _____

- rainy days _____

- days altogether _____

✤ Make your own weather chart for a month using Class 3's symbols.

Sunday							
Monday							
Tuesday							
Wednesday							
Thursday							
Friday							
Saturday							

Favourite sports

Name _____

Favourite sports

Class 5 have done a survey. They asked every child in the class about their favourite sport. They recorded the data and made a graph.

football	ⅢⅢ ⅢⅠ
judo	ⅢⅠ
rounders	ⅢⅢ
swimming	ⅢⅢⅢ ⅢⅠ
tennis	Ⅱ

❖ How many children are there in the class?

_____

❖ What is the favourite sport?

_____

❖ Do you think this sport would be the favourite in your class? Carry out a survey like Class 5's to find the favourite sports in your class.

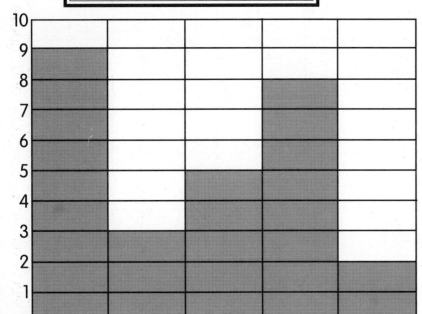

Name _____

Hair and eyes

The children in Class 5 have been collecting data about hair and eye colour.
They chose several different ways in which to record the information.

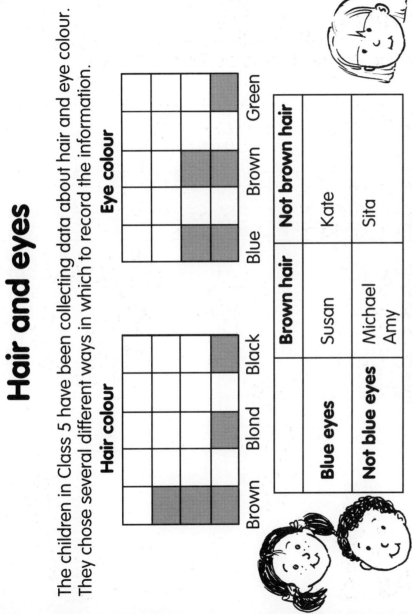

Hair colour

	Brown	Blond	Black

Eye colour

	Blue	Brown	Green

	Brown hair	Not brown hair
Blue eyes	Susan	Kate
Not blue eyes	Michael Amy	Sita

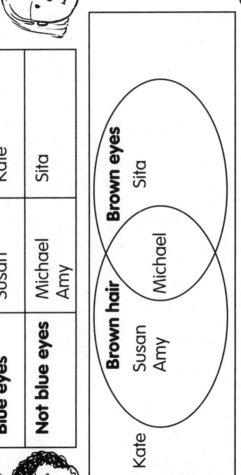

Brown hair — Susan, Amy, Michael

Brown eyes — Michael, Sita

Kate

❖ Complete these descriptions using this data:

● Susan has _____ eyes and _____ hair;

● Michael has _____ eyes and _____ hair;

● Amy has _____ eyes and _____ hair.

❖ Which children have got brown hair?

❖ What do you know about Kate?

❖ What do you know about Sita?

❖ Collect data from your group and choose a way to record the information.

Name _____

Pet count

Opposite is a pet picture graph. It shows the pets of children in Class 3. If a child had more than one pet, they chose their favourite for the graph.

❧ Answer these questions about Class 3's graph.
- How many children are there in Class 3?
- Which pet is the most popular?
- How many children have a rabbit?

❧ Now collect some information from your class about pets. Decide whether to include all the children's pets or just each one's favourite.

❧ Make your own picture graph to show the data you have collected.

❧ Think of some questions you could ask about your graph.

Pet count

Class 3's pet graph

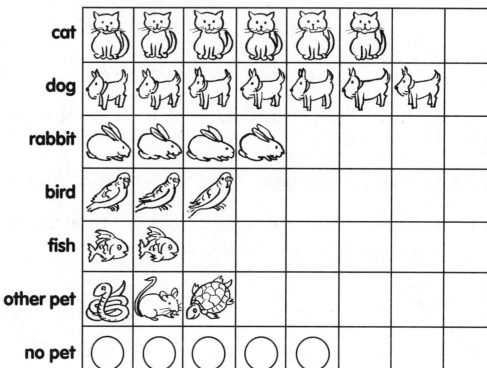

Name _____

Shape Venn

You will need some solid shapes like these:

cube   **cuboid**   **triangular prism**   **cone**   **sphere**   **cylinder**

❖ Look at the Venn diagrams below. For each solid shape in turn, look at the statements in the circles and decide if you can write the name of the shape in a circle.

❖ Put the name of the shape in the space where the circles overlap if it fits both statements.

❖ Make up some Venn diagrams of your own for sorting shapes. Can you use three overlapping circles?

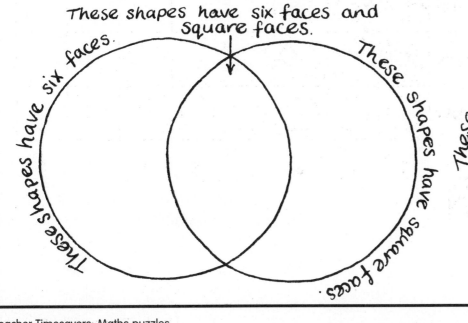

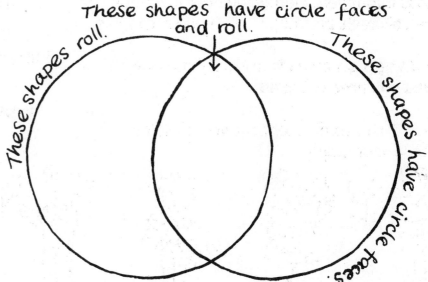

Party time

Name _____

Party time

Six children, three pairs of brothers and sisters, are invited to a party. Ben and Becky Blue are brother and sister, Rick and Rachel Red are brother and sister and Gary and Gail Green are brother and sister.

❧ Can you arrange the children around the table so that:
• no boys sit next to each other;
• no girls sit next to each other.

❧ Is there more than one way of arranging the seats?

❧ What happens if you also decide that :
• no brother and sister may sit next to each other?
• no brother and sister may sit opposite each other?

❧ Investigate all the seating plans!

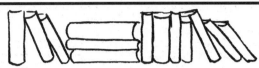

Book count

Grange School book count

Grange School have been doing a book count. They have recorded the data on a graph.

The symbol 📘 stands for 10 books.

📖 shows less than 10.

❧ About how many books are there in Class 2?

❧ About how many books are there altogether?

❧ Could you organise a book count in your school? Start with your own class.

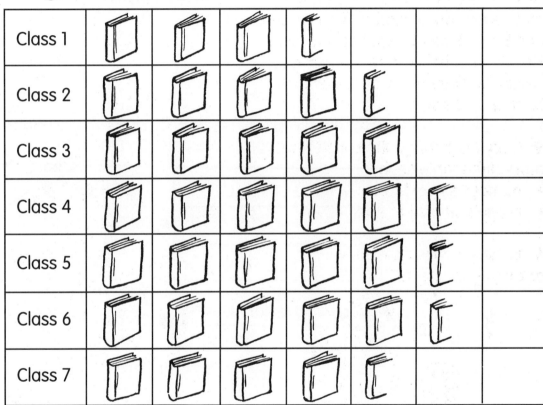

📘 = 10   📖 = less than 10

Shape tree

Name _____

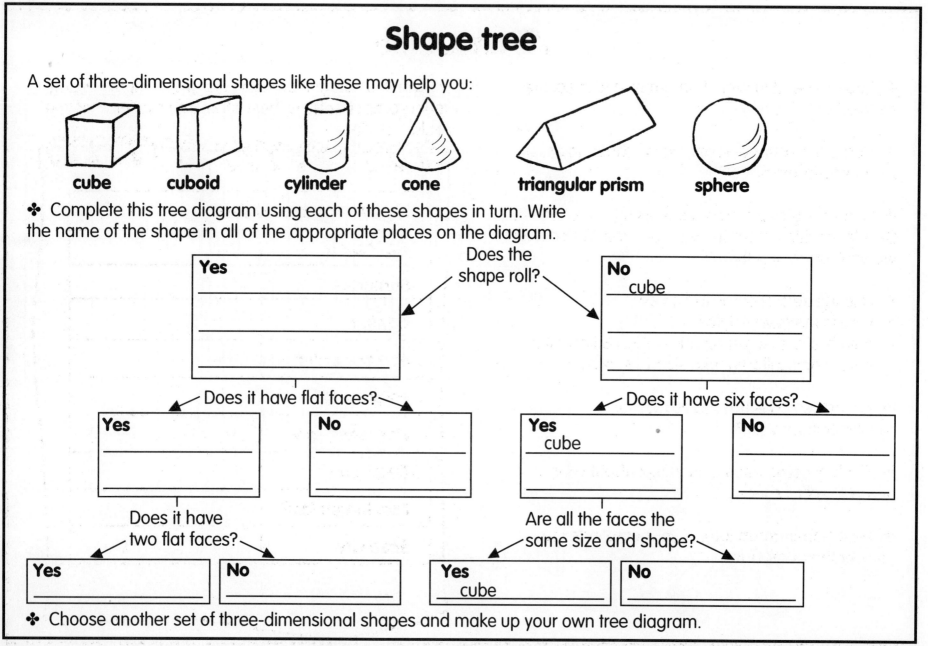

Shape tree

A set of three-dimensional shapes like these may help you:

cube **cuboid** **cylinder** **cone** **triangular prism** **sphere**

♣ Complete this tree diagram using each of these shapes in turn. Write the name of the shape in all of the appropriate places on the diagram.

Does the shape roll?

Yes
_____
_____
_____

No
cube
_____
_____
_____

Does it have flat faces?

Yes
_____
_____

No
_____
_____

Does it have six faces?

Yes
cube
_____
_____

No
_____
_____

Does it have two flat faces?

Yes
_____

No
_____

Are all the faces the same size and shape?

Yes
cube
_____

No
_____

♣ Choose another set of three-dimensional shapes and make up your own tree diagram.

All about me

❖ You will need to work in a group and measure each other.

❖ Complete your personal record sheet and stick it on to cardboard.

❖ Use your group's record sheets for a card index. Decide in which order to sort the cards. Which fields will you use to sort them?

❖ Use the sets of cards to find out:
• who is the tallest child?
• how many children are older than 85 months?
• how many children take size 13 shoes?

❖ Is it easier to re-sort the groups for different information?

❖ Think of some questions to ask about your group's record sheets.

❖ Let another group look at your card index to answer the questions.

❖ Can you set up a database for the computer using your record sheets? Is there other information that you could include?

My personal record sheet	
First name	
Surname	
Boy/girl	
Age in months	
Height (cm)	
Handspan (cm)	
Cubit (cm)	
Foot length (cm)	
Shoe size	

Name _____

Triple cones

Tommy sells triple cones of ice-cream, each contains three scoops. He sells strawberry, chocolate and lemon flavours.

❧ How many different combinations of three scoops can he sell? Use three different-coloured pencils, to colour in these ice-cream cones to find out.

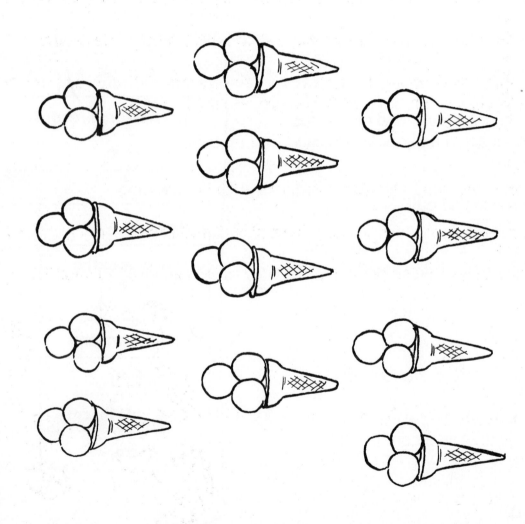

You may not need to colour in all these cones.

❧ What happens if he adds an extra flavour, for example orange? Investigate all the different combinations now.

Teacher Timesavers: Maths puzzles

Spinners

❧ Colour two segments of the spinner at the bottom of this page in blue and four in red.

❧ Cut out the spinner and stick it on to card. Push a short pencil through the centre.

❧ Play this game with a friend, taking it in turns to spin the spinner: if it lands on a red segment your friend wins, if it lands on a blue segment, you win. Have 20 spins each.

❧ Do you think this is a fair game?

❧ How can you change the game to make sure that it is fair?

❧ Can you make a spinner that is fair if three people play? What about four players, or more?

❧ Investigate different spinners and play games with them. Record what you notice.

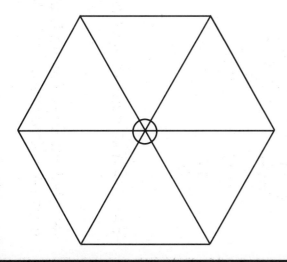

Fixture list

 Fixture list

Four football teams decided to form a league: West United, East Rovers, North Town and South Albion. In one season, each team will play all the other teams twice, once at home and once away.

✤ How many matches will each team play?

_____

✤ How many matches will be played altogether?

_____

Another club, Compass Athletic, decides to join the league.

✤ How many matches will they have to play?

_____

✤ How many matches will now be played altogether?

_____

The English Premier League has 22 teams.

✤ How many matches will, say, Manchester United play in the league each season?

_____

✤ How many matches will be played altogether in the Premier League in one season?

_____

More or less?

Here is some information about the children in a group.

Name	Height	Brothers/sisters	Wears glasses
Ajit	150cm	1 sister	No
John	148cm	2 brothers	Yes
Martin	142cm	1 of each	No
Ian	153cm	None	No
Sushila	144cm	2 sisters	No
Elizabeth	136cm	None	Yes
Luke	146cm	2 brothers	No
Charlotte	155cm	1 brother	No

✤ If the children in this group stand in a circle and another child, Richard, stands in the middle, blind-folded, is he more likely to point to:

• a boy or a girl? _____

• a child over 150cm or under 150cm? _____

• a child who wears glasses or a child who does not wear glasses? _____

• a child with brothers and sisters or an only child? _____

• a child with four letters or less in their name or a child whose name has more than four letters? _____

New shoes

New shoes

In interpreting data, the words **range**, **median** and **mode** are often used. The **range** is calculated by finding the difference between the highest and lowest number in the data. The **median** is the middle point, the **mode** is the most popular item and the **mean** is the average value.

These are the numbers of each different size of men's shoes sold in a shoe shop during one Saturday:

Men's shoe sizes	7	$7\frac{1}{2}$	8	$8\frac{1}{2}$	9	$9\frac{1}{2}$	10	$10\frac{1}{2}$	11	$11\frac{1}{2}$	12
Number of customers	5	1	12	18	24	19	15	14	8	6	3

✤ Record the information about shoe sales shown in the table above on the graph opposite.

✤ What is the range of sizes? _____

✤ What is the median size? _____

✤ What is the mode? _____

✤ What is the mean? _____

✤ How might this data help the shoe shop manager?

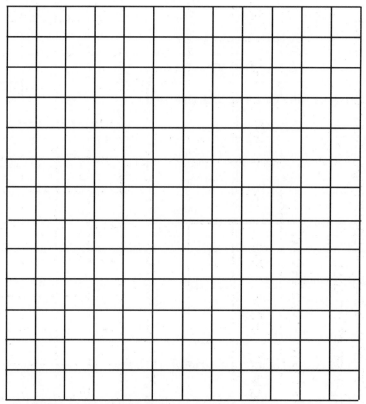

Name _____

Ready reckoner

Chocolate costs 30p for 50g. A shopkeeper decides to make a 'ready reckoner' of the cost.

♣ Complete his reckoner below:

Chocolate (g)	50	100	150	200	250	300
Cost (p)		60			150	

♣ Mark the cost of each amount on the graph below:

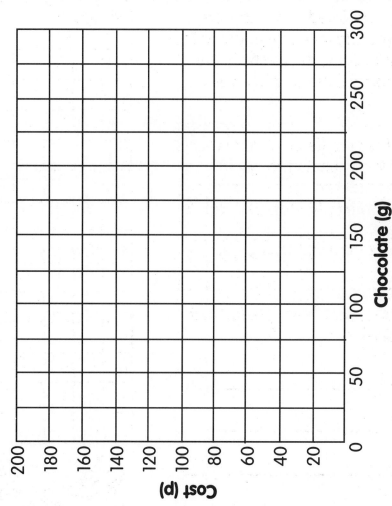

Cost (p)

200 180 160 140 120 100 80 60 40 20

0   50   100   150   200   250   300

Chocolate (g)

♣ Put a ruler along the points. What do you notice?

♣ Does 0 lie on this line? Why do you think this is?

♣ About how much would 175g of chocolate cost?

♣ About how much chocolate would you get for 40p?

♣ Choose a subject for your own 'ready reckoner'.

Tallying

Tallying

Tallying is a simple system which can be used to collect large amounts of data easily. In a tally system:

I	means one item,
II	means two items,
III	means three items,
IIII	means four items,
ЖΉ	means five items....

These tally charts show the number of people using a pedestrian crossing during three periods in a day.

8.00 am / 9.00 am	
Adults	ЖΉ ЖΉ ЖΉ ЖΉ ЖΉ ЖΉ ЖΉ ЖΉ ЖΉ ЖΉ II
Children	ЖΉ ЖΉ ЖΉ ЖΉ ЖΉ I

1.00 pm / 2.00 pm	
Adults	ЖΉ ЖΉ ЖΉ ЖΉ ЖΉ ЖΉ ЖΉ ЖΉ ЖΉ ЖΉ ЖΉ ЖΉ IIII
Children	ЖΉ ЖΉ ЖΉ I

6.00 pm / 7.00 pm	
Adults	ЖΉ ЖΉ ЖΉ ЖΉ ЖΉ ЖΉ ЖΉ ЖΉ ЖΉ ЖΉ ЖΉ ЖΉ
Children	ЖΉ II

♣ Convert the information shown into graphs.

♣ Now answer these questions.
• How many children use the crossing altogether?

_____

• How many adults use the crossing altogether?

_____

• Which time do most adults use the crossing?

_____

• Which time do most children use the crossing?

_____

• Which time is the busiest overall?

_____

♣ Discuss the reasons for your answers.

Name _____

Table repeats

The digital root of a number is the single digit you eventually get to by repeatedly adding together the digits in the original number.

For example: if the number is 24, adding the digits 2 + 4 gives a digital root of 6; or 98 gives 9 + 8 = 17, so 1 + 7 gives a digital root of 8.

❖ Investigate the times tables to see if there are any patterns in the digital roots of the answers. Try the three times and six times tables first.

❖ Look at the other times tables in the same way.

Three times table	
Number	Digital root
3	3
6	6
9	9
12	3
15	6
18	9

Six times table	
Number	Digital root
6	6
12	3
18	9
24	6

❖ Does the pattern continue?

❖ Does the pattern continue?

Heads and tails

 # Heads and tails

You will need: a coin.

When a coin is tossed it is equally likely to come down 'heads' or 'tails'.

✣ Work with a partner and predict how many 'heads' and how many 'tails' you would expect if you tossed the coin ten times. If you tossed the coin 100 times, how many 'heads' and how many 'tails' would you expect?

✣ Now test this out. Toss the coin ten times and ask your partner to record the results in the first column.

Toss	Results
1	
2	
3	
4	
5	
6	
7	
8	
9	
10	

✤ How many times did you get 'heads' and how many times did you get 'tails'?

_____

✤ Now ask your partner to toss the coin ten times while you record the results in the second column. Are your results similar?

_____

✤ Increase the number of times you toss the coin. Try 20, 50 and 100 times. Record your results.

✤ What do you notice about the results?

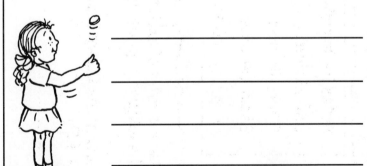 

_____

_____

_____

_____

Name _____

Exchange rates

You can find out how much £1 is worth in different currencies from most newspapers. This is the 'rate of exchange'.

Rates for travellers

USA (dollars)	1.55
France (francs)	9.16
Spain (pesetas)	216.00
Germany (marks)	2.71

♣ Use the rates of exchange given above to work out the following questions. You could use a calculator to help you.

● How many **francs** were received for:

1 £50 _____ 2 £150 _____ 3 £400? _____

● How many USA **dollars** were received for:

1 £100 _____ 2 £350 _____ 3 £500? _____

● How many **marks** were received for:

1 £80 _____ 2 £450 _____ 3 £1000? _____

♣ Imagine that you are going to Spain for two weeks for your holiday. Decide how much money you will take. How many **pesetas** will this be worth?

At the dentist

At the dentist

Statement: the children who eat the most sweets have the most fillings done at the dentist's.

♣ Is this statement true? To find out you will have to collect data.

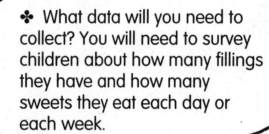

♣ What data will you need to collect? You will need to survey children about how many fillings they have and how many sweets they eat each day or each week.

♣ Other decisions to make may include:
• how many children you need to survey;
• how you can record the sweets eaten – by the number of bars or the number of grams perhaps;
• how you can show the data best.

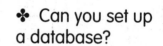

♣ Can you set up a database?

♣ Interrogate your data. Is the statement true?

Name _____

Pie charts

The **pie chart** is another way of showing information.

This pie chart shows how children travel to school.

* Which is the most popular way to travel?

* Which is the least popular?

* Complete the table below to show how you spend your day. The figures are the total number of hours spent doing each activity.

	school	playing	watching TV	eating	bed	other things
Jo	7	2	4	1	8	2
Me						

* Use both sets of figures to complete the pie charts to show how you and Jo use your time.

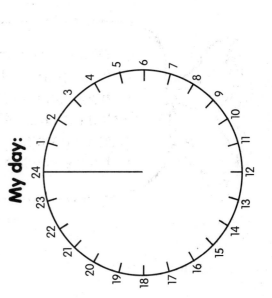

Jo's day:

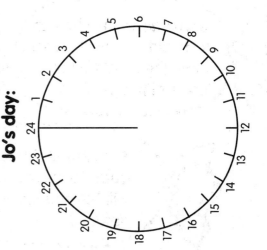

My day:

Venn diagrams

Venn diagrams

This is a type of graph called a **Venn diagram**. It shows a number of sets of information together.

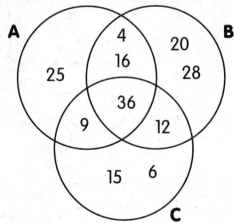

In this Venn diagram the numbers used are: 4, 6, 9, 12, 15, 16, 20, 25, 28 and 36. They are divided into three sets:

A = (square numbers)
B = (multiples of 4)
C = (multiples of 3)

(A square number is made by multiplying a number by itself, for example 5 × 5 = 25. A multiple of, say, 4 is any number made by multiplying by 4. So 20 is a multiple of 4, since 4 × 5 = 20.)

✤ Use the information in the Venn diagram to answer the following questions.

• Which number is a square number only?

_____

• Which numbers are multiples of 4 only?

_____

• Which numbers are multiples of 3 only?

_____

• Which numbers are multiples of 4 and square numbers?

_____

• Which numbers are multiples of 3 and square numbers?

_____

• Which numbers are multiples of 3, 4 and square numbers?

_____

Name _____

Happy birthday

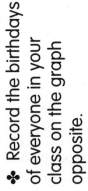

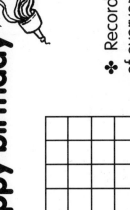

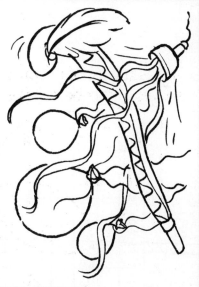

✤ Record the birthdays of everyone in your class on the graph opposite.

♣ Why are the spaces numbered and not the lines?

✤ Are more children born in the first half of the year?

✤ Are more children born in the summer than in the winter?

✤ Which month is most popular?

♣ Which month is least popular?

✤ Are any of the children in the class 'birthday twins' and have their birthdays on the same day?

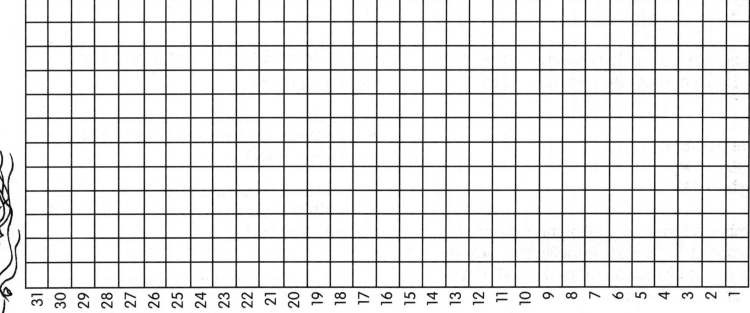

	December	November	October	September	August	July	June	May	April	March	February	January

31 30 29 28 27 26 25 24 23 22 21 20 19 18 17 16 15 14 13 12 11 10 9 8 7 6 5 4 3 2 1

Curved graphs

Name _____

Curved graphs

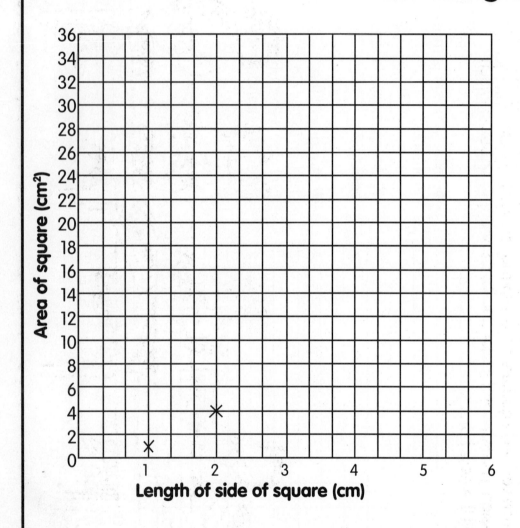

✤ Complete the table below and then mark the points on the graph.

Length of side of square	1	2	3	4	5	6
Area of square						

✤ Join the points with a smooth curve.

✤ Use the graph to find the areas of squares with sides:
- $2\frac{1}{2}$ cm;
- $3\frac{1}{2}$ cm;
- $4\frac{1}{2}$ cm.

✤ Find the length of the side of a square which has an area of:
- 5cm;
- 15cm;
- 20cm.

✤ Check your answers by using a calculator.